SCRAPBOOK
memorabilia

Safe and Unique Ways to Showcase Your Life's Mementos

Amy & Joani

Tim & Matt

THE BOXCAR CHILDREN

Photo 2005

PENNSYLVANIA

P.R.R. 76975

How our kids became The Boxcar Children

Cori Dahmen

MEMORY MAKERS BOOKS

Denver, Colorado

AUTHOR AND ARTIST CORI DAHMEN

Managing Editor MaryJo Regier
Art Director Nick Nyffeler
Photographer Ken Trujillo
Art Acquisitions Editor Janetta Abucejo Wieneke
Craft Editor Jodi Amidei
Graphic Designers Jordan Kinney, Robin Rozum
Production Coordinator Matthew Wagner
Contributing Photographers Camillo DiLizia, Jennifer Reeves
Editorial Support Karen Cain, Amy Glander, Emily Curry Hitchingham, Dena Twinem
Contributing Memory Makers Masters Diana Hudson, Kelli Noto, Denise Tucker, Angelia Wigginton

Published by Memory Makers Books, an imprint of F+W Publications, Inc.
12365 Huron Street, Suite 500, Denver, CO 80234
Phone (800) 254-9124

First edition. Printed in the United States.
10 09 08 07 06 5 4 3 2 1

Library of Congress Cataloging-in-Publication Data

Dahmen, Cori, 1965-
Scrapbook memorabilia : safe and unique ways to showcase your life's mementos / Cori Dahmen.
96 p. cm. : ill
Includes index.
ISBN-13: 978-1-892127-76-1
ISBN-10: 1-892127-76-8
1. Photograph albums. 2. Scrapbooks. 3. Souvenirs (Keepsakes) I. Memory Makers Books. II. Title

TR501.D34 2006
745.593--dc22

2005057667

Distributed to trade and art markets by
F+W Publications, Inc.
4700 East Galbraith Road, Cincinnati, OH 45236
Phone (800) 289-0963

Distributed in Canada by Fraser Direct
100 Armstrong Avenue
Georgetown, ON, Canada L7G 5S4
Tel: (905) 877-4411

Distributed in the U.K. and Europe
by David & Charles
Brunel House, Newton Abbot,
Devon, TQ12 4PU, England
Tel: (+44) 1626 323200,
Fax: (+44) 1626 323319
E-mail: mail@davidandcharles.co.uk

Distributed in Australia by Capricorn Link
P.O. Box 704, S. Windsor NSW, 2756 Australia
Tel: (02) 4577-3555

Memory Makers Books is the home of *Memory Makers*, the scrapbook magazine dedicated to educating and inspiring scrapbookers. To subscribe, or for more information, call (800) 366-6465.
Visit us on the Internet at www.memorymakersmagazine.com

About the author

Combining a lifelong passion for scrapbooking with a love of saving little items to help preserve special memories, Cori Dahmen brings her own ideas and insight to the topic of scrapbook memorabilia. Her professional scrapbooking experience includes a brief stint working at a retail scrapbook store, teaching classes and creating designs for product manufacturers and at trade shows. Cori is also a published author and contributor to both *Memory Makers* magazine and Memory Makers Books. She and her family call the great northwest home; they live in beautiful Washington State.

This book is dedicated to some of the most amazing and talented scrapbookers in the world:

Diana Hudson • Pam Kopka • Shelley Laming • Kelli Noto
Elizabeth Ruuska • Denise Tucker • Angelia Wigginton

Without your insight, help and dedication, this book would not have been possible.

Thanks also to my husband, Brian, and our four children, for help with all the mundane chores that consume so much of my time. Without your extra effort, the roof would definitely have fallen in.

To the generous and friendly scrapbook-supply companies that graciously donated product for this book, a huge and heartfelt thanks. You are much appreciated.

Carolee's Creations • Colorbök • Creative Imaginations
Krylon • Paper Loft • Pebbles • QuicKutz, Inc. • SEI

Table of contents

PAGE 23

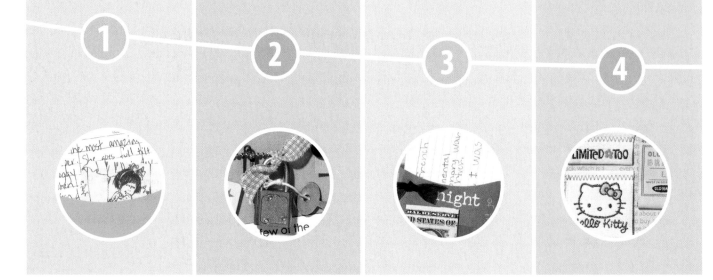

PAGES 12-19
BACKGROUNDS
Featuring clever ways for using memorabilia as scrapbook page backgrounds

PAGES 20-27
TIE-ONS
Showcasing ideas for tying or attaching souvenirs and mementos onto scrapbook pages

PAGES 28-37
POCKETS & POUCHES
Displaying innovate concepts for creating your own pockets or pouches to hold precious keepsakes

PAGES 38-45
EMBELLISHMENTS
Spotlighting smart approaches for using memorabilia as one-of-a-kind page embellishments and accents

1   2   3   4

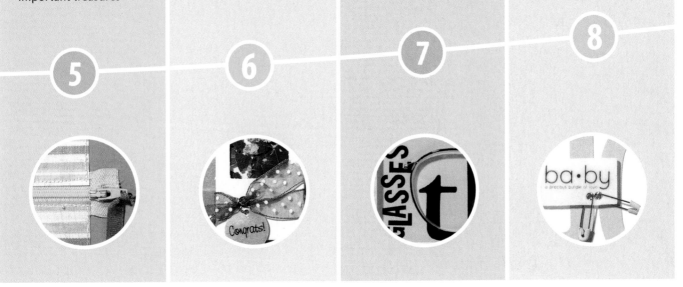

testify to LOVE

When I was a teenager and I fell in "love" that feeling took over all my thoughts and I'd scribble my initials, linked in a heart, with whoever I was in "love" with at that time, all over the covers of my notebooks. In college I met Christ and I learned about eternal "love" and what that meant in all our lives. Also during college I met the "love" of my life, my best friend and husband, Brian. Once again I learned that "love" was so much bigger, deeper, stronger and more encompassing than I'd ever imagined. Then I had babies and the "love" I felt for those tiny new pieces of my heart was different than any I'd ever experienced. In my early 30's I joined a women's bible study, and the topic for that group was "love"; it's meaning, how we experienced it, how we accepted what it meant and how it changed us. It was then that I learned that no one "love" is more important or precious than any other. Each "love" we experience is valuable and treasured for it's own sake and that each "love" makes us complete as a person. Each aspect of love takes over a small, or a large, section of our heart and makes a home there. All our loves are important. All shape our present and our future. All make us who we are.

Forever

THE LIVING BIBLE

Introduction

Hello! Welcome to the joy and fun of putting scraps from your lives into your memory albums. As I pull together elements for scrapbook pages, I find myself continually going to my memorabilia drawers and jars. The little trinkets I save represent many of the most pivotal and cherished elements from my past and present. Items that would often be meaningless to others help me express my feelings about the people and things I love the most. And that's what incorporating memorabilia into your scrapbook albums can do for you.

In this book, you will learn all about proper preservation techniques to ensure your memorabilia is ready for the archival protective environment of scrapbook albums. You will also discover how to include memorabilia in innovative layouts as backgrounds and embellishments or feature it in easy-to-make pockets, pouches, envelopes, enclosures, shakers and frames. From these ideas, you can then explore ways to bring your memorabilia to life in baby, holiday, school, vacation, wedding albums and more.

Using memorabilia will help you realize how much personality and life is added to the scrapbook page because of their inclusion. I hope you will also find the joy, warmth and reality that memorabilia brings to completed layouts, making your albums even more meaningful.

Cori

Top 10 tips for saving and using memorabilia

There are many good reasons to save memorabilia, keepsakes and mementos that are important to us—even if the items are important to us for just a brief period in time. Likewise, there are also a few good things to keep in mind when using these items in your scrapbook albums.

1 Save the important stuff. If it's not important, let it go.

2 If the pictures are the last thing noticed, something is wrong.

3 Let saved items help tell the story. The real story. The good, the bad and the ugly.

4 Don't lose focus of why you do this.

5 Little moments and tiny treasures often make the most lasting memories.

6 Anything goes. If you like it, do it.

7 Stretch your imagination. If you want to save an item, you can.

8 The most common and frequently saved items can be shown in fun and unique ways.

9 The items you save help identify and personalize the elements that are the sum of a person, event or memory.

10 Every page you create can't be your favorite, but it can and should make you smile.

Getting started

In the next few pages, you will learn about using different types of memorabilia safely and effectively in your scrapbook albums, as well as the tools and supplies that make adding memorabilia a snap.

WHAT IS MEMORABILIA?

In the dictionary, it is described as "things worth remembering or recording, as a collection of anecdotes, accounts, etc., or of mementos, especially about one subject, event, etc." In plain English, memorabilia is anything YOU want it to be. If an item or series of items makes you think of a time, place or event, it is memorabilia. Too often the idea of "real" memorabilia can bog you down and get you lost in the deception of generalizations. Postcards, school art and baby felicitations certainly make up a good portion of what we generally consider memorabilia, but true memorabilia is so much more than that. It is the plastic ring from a cigar wrapper that you were given in lieu of an engagement ring. It is the note your first boyfriend wrote to you back in the sixth grade. It is the tag from your favorite Beanie Baby. It is any item that matters to you or to someone that you love. It is anything you choose to save.

ARCHIVAL TERMINOLOGY

If you're already a scrapbooker, you're familiar with terms such as "acid-free," "lignin-free," "buffered" and "archival." All those essentially lead to the same principle: In order to be as long-lasting as possible, items that go into your albums need to be as safe as they can be. Photos and paper items naturally deteriorate over time. The rate at which they deteriorate can be increased or decreased based on the way they are stored or preserved. Acid and lignin, both found naturally in paper products, will increase the rate of decay of your photos and treasures. Using buffered paper (which helps control the pH of paper over time) and albums that are free of or protected from those elements will increase the longevity of your scrapbooks. If you're concerned about the amount of acid in any paper product, check the levels with a pH pen. Follow the manufacturer's guidelines on the packaging for safe ranges and levels.

If items are found to be unsafe, treat them with a preservation spray, again following manufacturer's instructions. Inks and dyes vary in how colorfast they are and how long they resist fading.

Pigment-based ink (rather than dye-based ink), found both in printers and in stamping ink, is less likely to run, smear or fade over time. When mounting or storing memorabilia in plastic, use products that are made of polypropylene, polyethylene or polyester. Never use items made from PVC (vinyl, or polyvinylchloride); it can produce a gas and can damage your treasures. Different metals can react to paper and photographs, so it is generally best to use metals that have been coated. Saving plants and flowers can be meaningful and fun, but be sure to use caution and enclose them completely as they contain lignin, which can stain paper.

STORAGE OF PHOTOS AND MEMORABILIA

Where you store your photos and memorabilia is equally important. Areas of intense heat or cold can damage paper items, and high humidity or moist environments cause paper to warp. The way you store your albums can also cause damage. Albums should be stored like books, with the spine up. Albums that are stored on their backs or faces tend to bow over time.

More preservation information

The Department of Paper Conservation at the J. Paul Getty Museum in Los Angeles, California, is a wonderful source of preservation information, as is the American Institute for Conservation of Historic and Artistic Works. Many common questions and concerns are addressed through the Web sites listed below:

www.aic-faic.org

www.imagepermanenceinstitute.org

www.scrapbookpreservationsociety.com

www.loc.gov/preserve/care/scrapbk.html

Basic *memorabilia information*

Here are a few simple yet important tips to keep in mind when saving, storing and showcasing memorabilia and ephemera in scrapbook albums:

O Assume all memorabilia to be acidic, and do not let it touch photos directly.

O Newspaper and many old paper documents and keepsakes are very acidic and full of lignin, but can successfully be saved in albums. Treating the clippings and documents with preservation spray (see photo above right) as soon as possible helps neutralize the acid and provides a buffer.

O Older newspaper clippings can be washed (see photo at bottom right), which helps even out the acid and increases the strength of the paper.

O Make second copies of irreplaceable documents by copying them onto acid-free, archival-safe paper stock. You can store or scrapbook the original and have a backup copy on a more stable type of paper. Consider photocopying historic documents onto oatmeal-colored paper to preserve the antique or heritage look.

O Store newspapers separately. Never store newsprint with other non-newsprint documents as the acidic nature of the newsprint may contaminate other documents. Store the newsprint in page protectors after it has been treated with an archival spray until ready to scrapbook.

O Store documents and memorabilia in a climate-controlled environment both before scrapbooking and once the memorabilia is in an album. Pick a cool, dark, dry place for the storage of these family treasures.

De-acidify memorabilia with a spray such as EK Success' Archival Mist before adding it to a scrapbook page. An alternative to spraying is to photocopy the news clipping or document onto acid-free paper.

O If your memorabilia item is too large to scrapbook, or you have storage-space limitations, consider photographing the items and getting rid of the original. This is a particularly good idea for 3-D school projects, sports trophies, band uniforms, military uniforms and bulky, homemade items of only slight sentimental value.

O Items comprised of fine particles and sharp items can scratch and damage both documents and photos. To store that type of item, make sure it is completely enclosed or encased in a protective covering (see photo at center right) before being included on your pages.

O Old fabric and lace is a joy but can easily disintegrate with time and handling. Take care to store very delicate items in a protective covering to prevent further deterioration.

Completely encapsulate memorabilia comprised of particulates or sharp edges in PVC-free (poly-vinylchloride) memory keepers to prevent photo scratches and damage to facing album pages.

To wash paper, simply soak it in a flat glass dish or stainless steel pan that contains distilled water. Completely immerse the paper, letting it soak for 15 to 30 minutes, then carefully smooth it out and allow it to lay flat until completely dry.

I made and mounted decorative bulletin boards in my daughter's bedroom as an organizational means for her to save the little things that are important to her. Not only can she see and enjoy saved items without creating clutter, when she replaces them with newer items, I use those bits of memorabilia as meaningful additions to the pages I make for her album.

Getting organized

I've had several people tell me that organizing saved items is the toughest part of using memorabilia in albums. Knowing which method is easiest and most effective for you, and what steps are needed to get piles of memorabilia in order so that they are easily accessible and usable, will serve you well. There are many storage options to suit available space, personality and budget restrictions. You can easily find a system that will work for you.

ACCORDION FILES

One of the most common and user-friendly options is an accordion-file folder. Those designed to hold 12 x 12" paper are generally ideal for scrapbookers as they are readily available, hold a wide assortment of items and are cost-effective. Most are available in a variety of fun colors and patterns, and some also come in smaller sizes so all types of memorabilia and photos can be stored in similar containers, making item identification, location and photo/memorabilia matching a simple task. The heavyweight paper used to separate the compartments is generally photo safe, but be sure to check the label when making your selection. The handle on top of the case makes it portable, and the slim design makes it easy to store. Each section has a tab at the top so labeling which types of items are in the individual compartments is a breeze.

STANDARD FILE FOLDERS

Another easy and common choice is standard file folders. They are economical, readily available and can be stored in file holders, specialty drawers or in plastic totes. Again, be sure to check the product information listed on the box to ensure the safety of your memorabilia. Most come in the standard 8½ x 11", but specialty scrapbook stores and manufacturers offer these in a 12 x 12" size. The benefit of this type of system is that you can add as many file folders as needed for the amount of saved memorabilia. The folders can be altered as needed without incurring too much cost or taking great amounts of time. Smaller pieces fit nicely in the folders when the sides are taped closed, and larger or flat pieces can be efficiently saved without any needed alterations. Generally this is less portable than the accordion system, but small file boxes and units with handles are plentiful.

PHOTO BOXES AND CLEAR TUBS

Even less expensive are photo boxes or clear plastic tubs. Rather than sorting memorabilia into categories or filing items into individual folders, you can toss them into these tubs and boxes and sort them later when you're ready to include the memorabilia on your pages. This method is much less time-consuming initially and acts as a localized storage place for all types of memorabilia. Each of my four children has a clear plastic tub with his or her name on it in the pantry. When they bring home schoolwork or awards or any item they'd like to save, it is put in their individual tub. While not as neat or tidy as the other systems, it is fast and easy and allows them to quickly and easily save the items of their choice.

Generations is one company that makes great memorabilia storage containers. Their system is called "Memory Express" (back row, center) and is available in most craft or scrapbook stores as well as on the Internet.

BASIC TOOLS AND SUPPLIES

Every scrapbooker should have, or have access to, a basic supply kit. This basic list can be expanded as needed for personal style and taste. But as a general rule, these items will be useful each and every time you scrapbook.

1 Clear ruler
2 Cutting mat
3 Eraser (not shown) and adhesive pick-up
4 Fine-point pen and pencil
5 Hole punch or piercing tool
6 Paper trimmer
7 Sharp craft knife
8 Sharp scissors
9 Tweezers
10 Wet and dry adhesives

ADDITIONAL TOOLS AND SUPPLIES

Scrapbookers who choose to include memorabilia in their albums will need a few more specific things. Here is a list of additional tools and supplies that you may need to hold, attach or incorporate these storage systems in your albums. With these supplies, any of the layouts in this book can be duplicated.

11 Brads, eyelets or pins
12 Dimensional mounting adhesive
13 Envelopes and enclosures
14 Foam core
15 Needle and thread or sewing machine
16 Preservation spray
17 Ribbon, twine or fiber
18 Spray adhesive
19 Super strong, dry adhesive (Super Tape by Therm O Web is shown)
20 Transparency, clear plastic or vellum

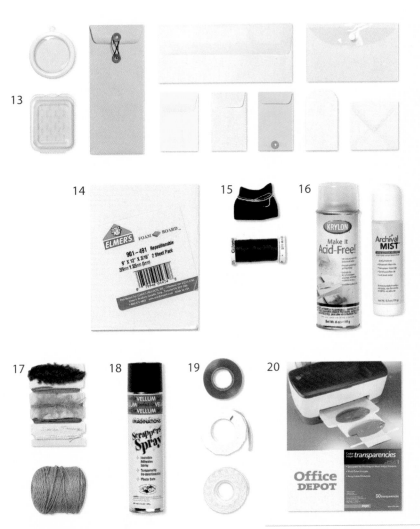

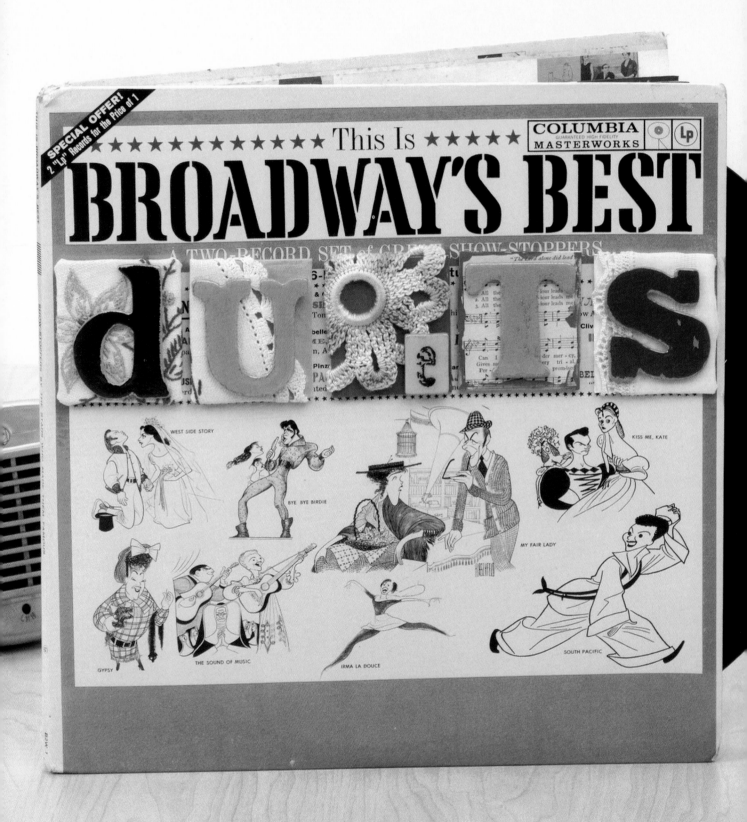

backgrounds

Memorabilia comes in numerous forms, and all kinds of saved items make great backgrounds for your scrapbook pages and memory projects.

The concept of using memorabilia as a background inspired the clever art piece shown on the left. The finished album is a masterpiece and beautifully shows exactly what I'm hoping to impart with this chapter: Memorabilia sets the stage for layout backgrounds, lending an authentic feel to scrapbook art.

Defining your saved piece is important when using it as part of the background, as you want to make sure the significance of the item is seen as memorabilia, rather than just a page accent. This chapter shows many techniques that work well in balancing the roles of memorabilia, stories and photos.

Become inspired by these fun ways to use memorabilia for page backgrounds. Let your imagination run wild and you will find that many seemingly everyday, nondescript items will work wonderfully to enhance your photos and memory projects.

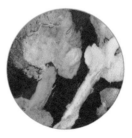  

Memorabilia for backgrounds

Here is just a small sample of some of the many memorabilia items that can be saved and used to create all or a portion of the background page:

- Artwork
- Autographs
- Baptism or confirmation documents
- Book or magazine pages
- Calendar pages and posters
- Canceled checks
- Candy and food wrappers
- Class outline or syllabus
- Expired official documents
- Fabric

- Flags
- Fliers and brochures
- Gift bags
- Greeting or gift cards
- Labels and tags from anything
- Lace and trim
- Letters and notes, both old and new
- Maps
- Menus
- Newspaper clippings

- Playing cards
- Postage-stamped envelopes
- Postcards
- Programs
- Receipts
- Ribbons
- School, sports and church awards
- Sheet music
- Trip tickets or permits

souvenir postcards

I'm pretty sure the number of post-cards Amy and I purchased during our special trip to the city exceeds the number of pictures we took. Since I didn't take pictures of every-thing we saw, I wanted to include the sightseeing highlights with post-cards. By layering and overlapping them to make a background, small glimpses of many of our favorite sights can be seen behind some of our favorite photos.

SAN FRANCISCO
Supplies: Letter stickers, metal word (K & Company); rub-on letters (Doodlebug Design); brads (Bazzill); ribbon (May Arts); cardstock

It was just Amy and I. Brian stayed home with the other kids while Bug & I flew to SF to see Auntie. It was our first trip back to the Bay Area since we'd moved and we "did" the city. Cable car ride, Fisherman's Wharf, China Town, the Golden Gate et all. I think the smiles seen in these photos says it all.

February 1996

autographs

We came back from Disneyland with four mini albums full of character signatures. How to save those in a more concise way presented a challenge until I decided they could be trimmed and used to make a background for the photos they represent. Not only does their use make the selection of background paper a breeze, it also clearly identifies each character.

GREETING FRIENDS
Supplies: Letter stickers (Chatterbox, Doodlebug Design); Mickey Mouse character sticker (Sandylion); cardstock

TIP Stitches act as a permanent anchor, holding assorted treasures firmly in place.

children's artwork

Cherished artwork, a picture and a little journaling make this simple page shine. By adding a favorite piece of her daughter's artwork to the layout, Shelley saved a piece of who her daughter was at that age. As Chandler grows and changes, her art is sure to change as well. Now she will always have a memento of what she created at age 8.

BUDDING ARTIST, Shelley Laming
Supplies: Gift wrap (Hallmark); letter stamps (Bunch Of Fun); photo corners (Heidi Swapp); chalk ink (Clearsnap); label sticker (Making Memories); cardstock; pen; staples

chandler, age 8

budding artist

Your art makes me happy!

school award and letter

Fortunately I didn't have any pictures of me in a swimsuit to accompany the award and block letter I was awarded. Since cheerleading had kept me from swimming on the team in previous years, it seemed natural to include a cheer picture on a page about being able to swim my senior year. The original block "P" is still gray and grungy and lives on my letterman's jacket, but this newly purchased one nicely enhances the layout about the story of how it was received.

PHS
Supplies: Patterned paper (Patchwork Paper Design); letter stickers (Chatterbox); ribbon (May Arts); mini brads (ScrapArts); cardstock; stamping ink

TIP Paper awards can often be cut down to include just the pertinent information. Photograph, color copy or scan the awards to reduce the size or to show them smaller on the page.

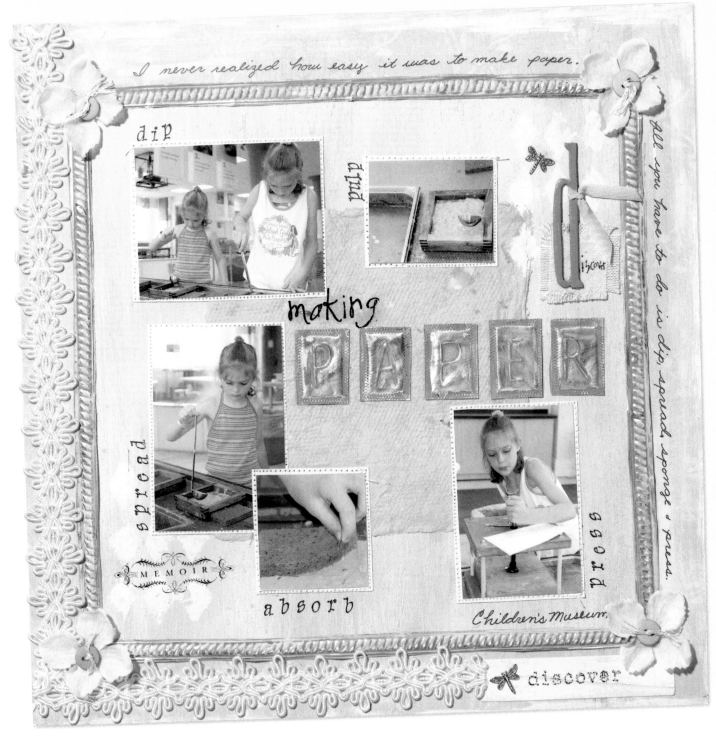

I never realized how easy it was to make paper.

dip

and

d discover

making

PAPER

spread

MEMOIR

absorb

press

Children's Museum.

discover

All you have to do is dip, spread, sponge, press.

handmade paper crafts

Using the paper the girls made at the time the photos were taken is a great visual enhancement that adds both fun and meaning to the page about the event.

MAKING PAPER, Pam Kopka
Supplies: Patterned papers (Bo-Bunny Press); rub-ons, chipboard letter, ribbon (Making Memories); diamond stamps (Wendi Speciale Designs); letter stamps (FontWerks); tags (Pebbles); dragonfly (Cut-It-Up); metal (Ten Seconds Studio); memoir rub-on (Creative Imaginations); cardstock; acrylic paint; ribbon; fabric; stamping ink

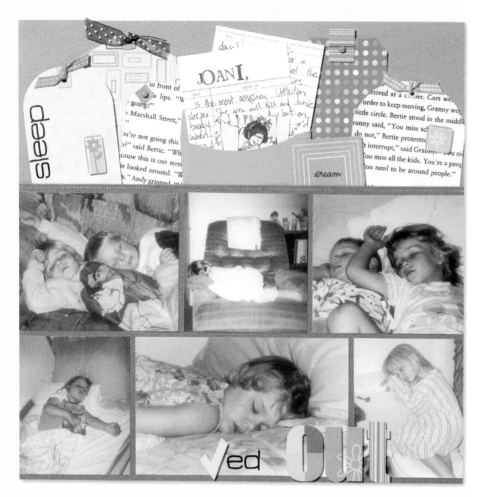

favorite old books

My darling daughter's propensity to fall asleep at the drop of a hat has caused many a book page to get wrinkled and torn. In fact, when we bought an old *Junie B. Jones* book at a yard sale, Joani cut out a picture of Junie and carried it around with her for a month or so. Using some of those saved, torn items here allows an older Joani the chance to see what her father and I love to remember.

CHECKED OUT

Supplies: Patterned papers, rub-ons, acrylic embellishments, die-cut letters (KI Memories); library pocket (Creek Bank Creations); tag toppers (QuicKutz); brads (Bazzill); ribbon (May Arts); letter stamps (PSX Design); tag templates (Accu-Cut); library cards (Boxer Scrapbook Productions); book pages (Junie B. Jones by Barbara Park); cardstock; stamping ink

 TIP Some types of memorabilia need to be saved in their entirety such as birth certificates, immigration papers and wedding licenses. Scan or photocopy and reduce in size to show in entirety on a scrapbook page.

dictionary page

That huge dictionary played an almost daily role in Kevin's life as he studied for a state-wide spelling bee. The use of a page from it here, as a background to the photo of Kevin poring over its contents, reinforces the dedication and determination to succeed seen on his young face.

UNABRIDGED, Kelli Noto

Supplies: Patterned papers (Paper Loft, Provo Craft); die-cut letters (QuicKutz); dimensional adhesive (JudiKins); mailing label (3M); stamping ink; ribbon; acrylic paint; dictionary page

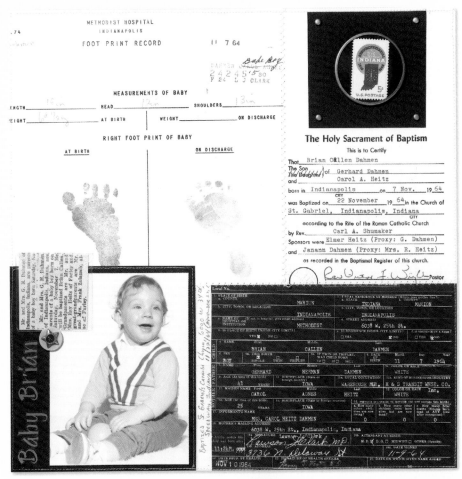

baby documents

Brian's mom was fantastic about saving bits and pieces from his baby days. Rather than making individual pages for each of the saved items, I included them all on one page in a collage format so none would be misplaced or overlooked. Each time my husband looks at the page, he notices something new and that allows him a chance to share yet another memory of his childhood with me and the kids.

BABY BRIAN
Supplies: Letter stickers (EK Success); clear pocket (Therm O Web); mini brads (ScrapArts); cardstock

maps

A section of a trail map combined with scenery photos sets an effective stage for memories of an outdoor trip. No pertinent or special information was below the trail line so I didn't feel the need to keep the map intact or create a pocket so the map could be pulled out. It simply adds to the story of the magnificent power that is Yosemite.

YOSEMITE
Supplies: Letter stickers (Creative Imaginations); mini brads (ScrapArts); ribbon (May Arts); bosher (Bazzill); cardstock

 TIP Items such as postcards, maps and pages from an old book enhance the finished piece yet don't need to be shown whole to achieve the desired effect.

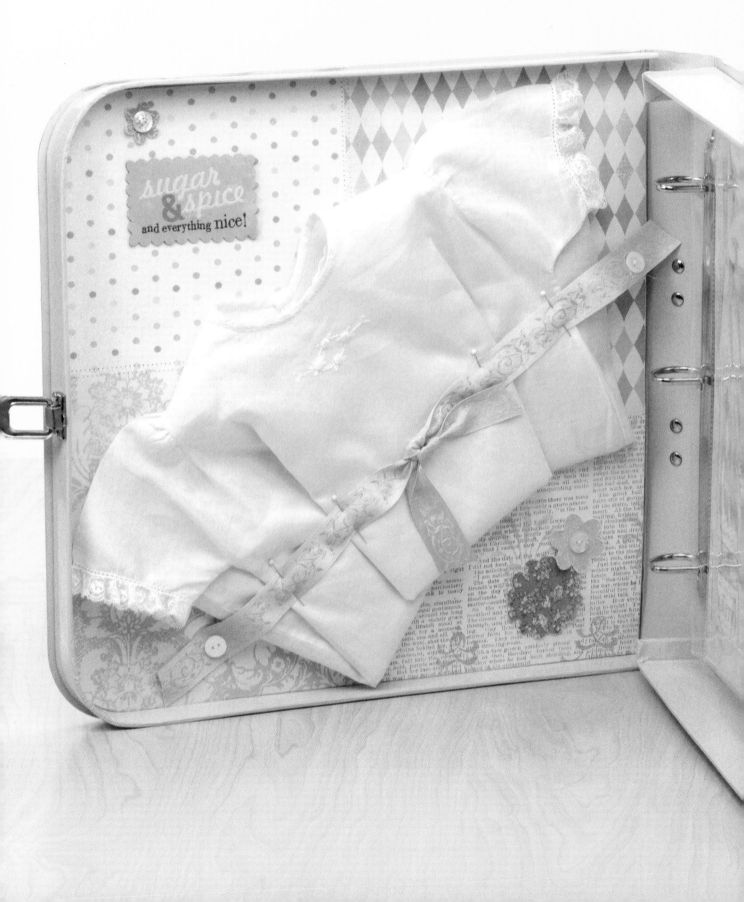

sugar
& spice
and everything nice!

tie-ons

Some memorabilia can become permanent, non-movable parts of your layouts—telling their story by becoming a lasting part of your page design. Other types of memorabilia are better suited to semipermanent display, adhered in a repositionable way in albums, like tying.

Ribbon easily holds memorabilia in place, yet can be untied for holding and viewing an item. Other items can be used to tie mementos and keepsakes on pages too. Clear fishing line or beading thread is inexpensive, long-lasting and works beautifully when something clear and less noticeable is desired. Twine, hemp and other types of cording also work well.

The choice you make about which type of ribbon or fiber to use will add to the overall feel of a page; try a variety of options before settling on one. However you choose to tie your memorabilia on a page, just remember that there are very few knots and bows that cannot be untied.

Memorabilia that can be tied on

Just about any small item imaginable can be tied onto a layout. Certainly, some things are more easily saved in pockets, pouches or envelopes, but most can be tied on, which offers a different look and feel to the work. Here are just a few items that work well when tied onto a layout:

- Buttons
- Cards and notes
- CDs and records

- Clothing and product labels
- Game pieces
- Jewelry and charms

- Ribbon-type awards
- Tools and hobby pieces
- Toy pieces

found trinkets

I am always finding trinkets and treasures in the bottom of my dryer. And the boys aren't even the worst culprits! Combining little pieces of their daily lives—strung on a found chain hanging between brads—with a beautiful yet silly photo of the girls allows me to share more than one story...to save more than one memory.

GIRL STUFF
Supplies: Frame, metal chain (Pebbles); ribbon (Beaux Regards); brads (ScrapArts); cardstock; stamping ink; jump rings

I guess we didn't walk a lot at home. In the city, with the schedules that accompany the daily grind, we just didn't.

But when we visited Grandma and Grandpa, Dad's parents, we walked. Up hills, down hills, on dirt roads, through fields and pastures, we walked and walked. And we talked. And I listened and learned from Dad.

He showed me how to identify different trees and bird calls. We chewed on sassafras sticks, tasting the pleasant flavor. I learned to imitate whippoorwills and bobwhites. I remember standing by still ponds, skipping rocks across the surface. We had contests. I never won.

I clamped my shoes down on empty beer cans and walked a half a mile with the aluminum "shoes" scraping annoyingly on the rocks. Dad taught me dubious tricks like how to blow my nose without a Kleenex-useful in emergencies when outside.

This was all before the interstate went through. We would visit them over teachers' institute in October and wouldn't hazard the journey again until April. We couldn't risk getting stuck in the mountains by snow.

Each trip, while similar, was special in its own way. I remember the April blooming in spring in Kentucky when we had left Indiana with winter coats on. I also remember being in Kentucky just as the sap flowed. That year, Dad and I walked and searched for small maple branches, about as thick as your finger. We cut lengths 8 or 9 inches long with a pocket knife. Back on Grandma's front porch, Dad scored the bark and carefully eased it off the branch. Notching out small parts, he carefully reassembled it all. And in a fit of Tom Sawyer-esque ingenuity, we each had small maple whistles. I always thought my dad could do anything in the world. And these little whistles proved it.

But age affects everything I guess. The whistles dried out and lost their song. Then grew so brittle, the mouthpiece split and fell apart. But I kept mine. This whistle is a symbol, a manifest memory of all those walks we used to take.

handmade toys

This touching and special layout shows how effective saving memorabilia in your albums can be. The story alone is poignant and powerful and one Elizabeth's children are sure to enjoy again and again. Yet adding the simple, old wooden whistle—attached with jute and jump rings—makes the page come to life. It adds depth and meaning to a tale already strong in its own right.

WALKS WE USED TO TAKE, Elizabeth Ruuska

Supplies: Patterned papers, zipper, jump rings, alphabet buttons (Junkitz); eyelets (Making Memories); ribbon (May Arts); chipboard letters (Li'l Davis Designs); cardstock

clothing buckles

Fashionista I am not. Comfortable overalls, a T-shirt and some flip-flops make me happy. When I have to wear dresses or pantyhose, I am uncomfortable and out of my element. I'm laid-back, casual and into comfort over style. Maybe not ideal from the standpoint of others, but that is who I am. In fact, I like my overalls so much that I have a hard time throwing them away when they are worn to the point of indecency. The only way I could bring myself to part with a favorite, yet completely worn out, pair of overalls was to save the strap and stitch it to my page. It helped me share the story of the role overalls play in my wardrobe, and the way some of my preferences have influenced the kids.

MADE FOR OVERALLS

Supplies: Patterned papers (Carolee's Creations); chipboard letter, ribbon buckles (Making Memories); rub-on letters (KI Memories); cardstock

made for OVERaLLs

Comfortable. Easy. like us. All reasons overalls, and do so, once in a while my off on the two of

Simple. Just I love to wear often. Every preferences rub you.

Fall 1996

heritage documents

Saved documents don't need to be displayed in entirety at all times, but they do need to be accessible and viewable when desired. Ribbon tied between eyelets holds old documents securely in place, yet can be untied so the papers can be viewed. Heritage photos can be tough to scrapbook, yet adding pertinent memorabilia to the layouts can save and share the photos and memories of yesterday in a convenient and effective way. I want my kids, as well as any future generations, to be able to see and feel who their ancestors were. These tangible pieces of their paternal grandmother's life can be easily learned from and explored at their convenience because they are saved in a useable and accessible way.

CAROL

Supplies: Patterned papers (Anna Griffin); ribbon (May Arts); die-cut letters (QuicKutz); circle punch (EK Success); cardstock; stamping ink

Born August 2, 1939 to Ray and Frances Heitz in Farley, IA Carol was the second of seven children. She lived on the family farm in Farley her entire childhood, moving to Los Angeles, CA when she married in 1963. She was helpful in caring for her younger siblings and she was very active in 4H. Some of the few pictures we have of young Carol show her involved in school, family and 4H events.

TIP If there is any doubt that you might want to remove or relocate an item at a later date, be sure to save it in a manner that allows it to be removed without destroying the page.

high-school diplomas

Ribbon corners make great anchors for holding letters and documents in place yet allowing them to be removed easily if needed. I can't imagine that we'll ever need to remove my mother-in-law's high-school diploma, but the ribbon allows us that option if needed or desired. Combining the diploma on a page with pictures of her at the same age helps make a complete statement and allows like items to be stored and enjoyed together.

'57 GRADUATE

Supplies: Patterned papers, ribbon corner, sticker (K & Company); metal clip, label holder (Making Memories); clock face (Li'l Davis Designs); die-cut letters (QuicKutz); metal word (Pebbles); word stamp (7 Gypsies); cardstock; stamping ink

1965

ANGEL

3. one tha...
good and beauti...
4. one sent to watch over
and protect; guardian

ANGELIC ANGELIA -- An angel took over for Mr. Stork and delivered this 8 - lb. 10 - oz. bundle from heaven to Zion-Benton Hospital. A dove - like coo and a heavenly smile won the hearts of Mr. and Mrs. William Harold Armstrong who claimed Angelia Maedean as their first "little bit of para-dise." They took her home to her first Cloud 9 at 2709 Elim, Zion. Mom, the former Bertha Maedean Hamm, heralded the January 11th arrival of their little cherub, and Mr. and Mrs. J. C. Hamm of Zion and Mr. and Mrs. Dayton Armstrong of Red Bay, Alabama, flew to catch a glimpse of their new little granddaughter.

newspaper birth announcements

By including the newspaper clipping of her birth announcement tucked beneath stitched ribbon, Angelia saved her own information in a beautiful and sentimental way. Little details are often the most important, and she has shared those here so future generations can benefit from them.

ANGEL, Angelia Wigginton

Supplies: Patterned papers (K & Company); ribbon (Offray); label holder, definition, ribbon slide, heart charm, metal letters, safety pins (Making Memories); vellum (Hot Off The Press); distress ink (Ranger)

 Using an extra-sticky and strong tape, such as Therm O Web's Super Tape, is an easy way to adhere ribbon of any type to your page or accent.

sundays, mondays

Four year old Jones. Lots of attitude, lots of fun. Every day, before school, she'd ask for the "Sundays, Mondays". That's how she referred to the weather page. She didn't care what the words said, she was looking at the pictures. The ones that told her that recess would be outside, that she could go swimming, that she could run in the sun.

1997

newspaper weather forecasts

Memorabilia doesn't have to be old or costly to be valuable. As a little girl, an important part of Joani's day was finding out what the weather forecast promised. She'd plan her own day, and everyone else's, around what the newspaper had to say. Because we live in the Pacific Northwest, there were many days when she was less than pleased about what she saw. She couldn't have cared less about anything else in the paper, but the "Sundays, Mondays" were a huge deal. I want to remember that time of her life, and I want her to be able to remember it as well. By punching holes in the page and inserting and wrapping ribbon, the folded weather reports are held neatly in place.

SUNDAYS, MONDAYS
Supplies: Patterned paper (Carolee's Creations); letter stickers, brads, tags, rub-on letters (Doodlebug Design); ribbon (May Arts); date stamp (Office Depot); cardstock

nails

The kids' first fort was as much fun for me as it was for them. They were diligent and worked so hard to make it exactly right. I laughed myself silly as I watched the younger kids grab more "nails" and pound away on those tiny picture-hanging brads. They did not want to hear that the brads weren't long enough. They were happy to be hammering and building. I couldn't make a layout about this event and not include some of the elements that brought me such merriment, adhered tidily in over-lapped and knotted ribbon.

BUILT STRONG TO LAST LONG...NOT
Supplies: Letter stickers (Mary Engelbreit); ribbon (May Arts); stencil template (Office Depot); rub-on numbers (Doodlebug Design); eyelets (Making Memories); cardstock

built strong
to last long...

NOT

The kids worked so hard on this fort, and they ALL had a blast building it! Matt started the project, asking if he could use the scrap lumber in our garage. He found old carpet, panels of plywood and all kinds of bits and pieces of wood. Once it started to take shape none of them could wait for it to be finished. While washing dishes one afternoon I looked out the window and saw Tim and Jones using these tiny, white, picture hanging nails. I laughed so hard I cried... the nails didn't go all the way through the wood, but as long as they were banging on something they were content. No one was more surprised then me when it didn't collapse the first time the kids entered it. We had to tear it down before summer was over as field mice thought the fort was pretty cool too.

••• 1998

TIP Clear fishing or beading filament could have been used to hold the clasp in place, but that might have caused it to look like it was floating off in space. The ribbon and brads anchor the clasp and add to the overall balance.

hardware

After climbing the YMCA rock wall at a local health fair, Matt started to ask for a metal clasp each time we went to the store. He received a pack in his stocking for Christmas and kept them clipped to his backpack for several years. Using a clip here, anchored by ribbon and brads, ties the two memories together and shows how one event can lead to another.

CLIMB HIGH
Supplies: Patterned papers (Doodlebug Design, KI Memories); letter buttons, brads (Doodlebug Design); ribbon (May Arts); clip (Target); cardstock; pen

It was like magic. As soon as we walked into the tent your eyes lit up. No doubt about it, you wanted to climb that wall. You were patient, you waited for your turn in a very long line and you did it. No problems. Piece of cake. I know that not all you want and hope for in life will come that easy, but I hope you approach all that truly matters with that same desire, fire and determination.

september 1997

pockets & pouches

Pockets and pouches are a popular way to store memorabilia on pages. They come premade and ready for embellishing or you can make charming, effective pockets and pouches with scraps you already have on hand to match any layout. Different from envelopes and enclosures, which can be closed or sealed off, pockets and pouches are open-ended and ready to hold whatever memorabilia items you wish to insert.

Pockets and pouches make the perfect page accents as they hold just about anything you can think of to save on a scrapbook page. They can be made to fit on any memorabilia project, and there is no item that will fit in an album that cannot be saved in a pocket or pouch.

Have fun experimenting with pockets and pouches, and be certain to use the strongest adhesives available—made specifically for scrapbooking—to ensure your pockets and pouches withstand years and years of memorabilia preservation and viewings.

Making pockets and pouches

Some of the many common items that can be made into pockets:

- Cardstock
- Cork paper
- Fabric
- Felt

- File folders
- Lace
- Page protectors
- Patterned paper

- Transparencies
- Tulle
- Vellum
- Woven ribbon

Attaching pockets and pouches

Pockets and pouches can be attached to your layouts in several different ways. For style variation, try these:

- Brads
- Buttons
- Eyelets

- Fiber or string
- Glue
- Ribbon

- Snaps
- Staples
- Super Tape

restaurant receipt stubs

My husband and I dated for three years before getting married, which amounts to a whole lot of date nights and dinners out. I'd saved all the receipt stubs from our favorite restaurants, and putting all those saved stubs on one layout, with one of the few dining photos we have, allows us to see and remember all those occasions. Because of the size and variety, it was easier to showcase them in several small pockets rather than one big one.

BON APPETITE

Supplies: Glassine envelopes (Little Black Dress Designs); embossed paper (K & Company); ribbon (Offray); die-cut heart (Heidi Swapp); brads (ScrapArts); die-cut letters, tag topper (QuicKutz); cardstock; stamping ink

used gift cards

Scrapbooking non-people layouts is tough for me, but important when sharing details of my daily life. Starbucks gift cards are a favorite of mine, both to give and receive, and I have saved several over the years. Business card pockets are the perfect showcase for these colorful keepsakes. They are important to me because they tell of times shared with my husband, children and friends. They show how I've influenced others and led them to the dark side of coffee addiction. They also show my kids just a little bit more about me.

ADDICTION IN A 16 OZ WHITE CUP
Supplies: Business card pockets (ACCO Brands); eyelets (Making Memories)

holiday photo cards

Saving the card and photo that we send out each Christmas has become a tradition as well as a challenge. The addition of a pocket to the layout about the photo shoot itself allows the large photo to take the limelight while letting the end result—the photo card—shine in its own right.

CHRISTMAS CARD PHOTO SHOOT
Supplies: Patterned papers (Flair Designs); die-cut letters, shapes (QuicKutz); wire (Westrim); eyelets (Making Memories); brads (ScrapArts); cardstock; pen

hidden memorabilia

Not all memorabilia has to be obvious to be included. Sometimes just having the memorabilia available and with a layout is the best way to save and store it. This large "hidden pocket"—created by sealing the side and lower edges of white cardstock on the organge background—holds brochures, pamphlets and the story of our trip to the aquarium. This allows several bold and colorful photos to be shown on one page without the distraction of multiple fliers and brochures.

AQUARIUM
Supplies: Acrylic letters (KI Memories); label maker (Dymo); brads (ScrapArts); cardstock

notecards and namesake mementos

This very simple page sure makes me smile. Speaking in public was a big deal for my youngest son, and he worked hard to make his speech special. We kept the notecards he referred to as well as his George W. props. Using two ready-made pockets layered together allowed me to keep and show all the memorabilia in one small space.

GEORGE W. THE FIRST

Supplies: Patterned papers (Chatterbox); letter stickers (Mustard Moon); rub-ons (Doodlebug Design, Making Memories); brads (ScrapArts); pocket (Creek Bank Creations); clear pocket (Therm O Web)

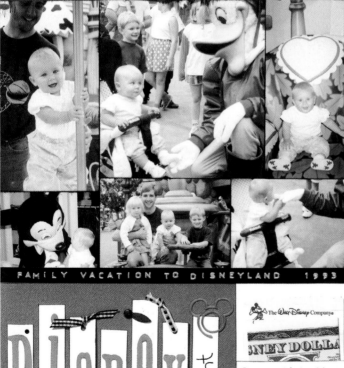

amusement-park souvenirs

My youngest daughter was not quite 9-months old on her first visit to Disneyland, and I wanted to save the entrance stub and Disney Dollar she received. A piece of folded-over cardstock made just the right pocket for this photo-packed page. There was no need to make multiple layouts about this one event as the story was comfortably told on a single layout.

DISNEY DELIGHT

Supplies: Letter stamps, eyelets (Making Memories); ribbon (May Arts); rub-on letters (Doodlebug Design); Mickey Mouse clip (EK Success); brad, photo turn (ScrapArts); label maker (Dymo); cardstock; acrylic paint; stamping ink

report cards and awards

Photos taken with teachers make an excellent page for storing report cards or special awards. The black-and-white photos keep the focus equally placed on all the photos, and Olivia will be able to pull out the report cards and awards any time she wants to see what she accomplished during that year.

MY TEACHER X 4, Angelia Wigginton

Supplies: Patterned paper (Basic Grey); ribbon, brads (Making Memories); letter stickers (Doodlebug Design, Sticker Studio); bottle cap (Mustard Moon); cardstock

silly yet sentimental souvenirs

Cardstock scraps inked and layered over each other form this pocket that holds some silly yet sentimental evidence of the fun we had on our camping trip. The saved pieces aren't necessary or even needed on the layout, yet they act as a visual reminder that fun can be had in the simplest of ways. Additional instructions are on page 92.

WHEN LIFE IS GOOD

Supplies: Rub-on letters (KI Memories); letter stickers (Scrapworks); wood letters (Westrim); ribbon (May Arts); brads (ScrapArts); cardstock; stamping ink

JUN 9 7

EASTER
BONNET
WHITE

MIXED

· PLaNTing smiles

It's not about the yard. It's not about
the flowers. It's not even about the
completed look. It's about the smiles
on the faces of those who got to help.

plant markers

The kids were quite proud of their planting efforts and wanted to
save the markers showing the names of the flowers they'd planted.
The small glassine pocket is perfect for holding them in place. They
can be pulled out and read or left alone in their little home.

PLANTING SMILES
*Supplies: Letter stickers (Making Memories); rub-on letters, buttons (Doodlebug
Design); glassine pocket (Little Black Dress Designs); brads (ScrapArts); date stamp
(Office Depot)*

Little Carol

Just a few pictures of dad's mom, Grandma Carol, from ages 2 to 6. In the one above you can see a bit of the Farley, IA farmhouse where she lived until getting married. On the back of the photo on the left she wrote "me when I was in the hospital for the first time". She had juvenile onset diabetes, which ultimately caused her early death. Her faith remained strong and these necklaces were among her few pieces of jewelry.

41-45

familial jewelry

My mother-in-law's jewelry was found in the boxes of documents left to us by my father-in-law. Not wanting the jewelry to stay in a box for another 20 years, I decided to combine her various crosses with assorted childhood photos. We can all now enjoy the presence of the little things that were important to her.

LITTLE CAROL

Supplies: Patterned paper (K & Company); hobby-card holders (Century); letter stickers (Doodlebug Design, K & Company); brad (ScrapArts); eyelet (Making Memories); photo corners (Canson); cardstock

TIP Photo tabs and tape-runner type adhesives are wonderful for mounting photos, as shown at the left, but they are generally not strong enough to hold heavier memorabilia such as heritage necklaces. PVC-free plastic pouches work better in this case.

memorial documents

When my father-in-law passed away, we got a few huge boxes of paperwork, postcards, letters, Mass cards and other assorted documents. The box included information about my mother-in-law, both of their parents and several relatives. Some of the documents were fragile and had to be saved carefully. A clear, PVC-free plastic pocket allows the items to be seen, yet keeps them safe. Additional instructions are on page 92.

PAPA GARY

Supplies: Patterned papers (Karen Foster Design); circle letters, clock pin, key, circle clasp (EK Success); chipboard letters (Rusty Pickle); ribbon (Beaux Regards); dimensional adhesive (JudiKins); cardstock; acrylic paint; stamping ink; page protector

PAPA GARY

For a man who loved to talk, he sure didn't say too much about himself. Brian and I asked him questions, many times, about his life in Wisconsin, and their move south to Marquette, IA. His dad, Gerhard Herman Sr. ran a mercantile, then a gas station and his mom stayed home with the boys, in their home above the shop. Both of his parents were older when he was born, and like many in that area, Catholic. The card in the pocket is one GH Sr. wrote to his sister, Catherine, right after Papa Gary was born. Included in the pocket are his Certificate of Baptism and birth certificate.

GH Dahmen

19"2$4

We is always better than I

Since our first date my most favorite place to be is, and has been, with you. Taking long walks. Riding bikes. Driving through the country. Listening to music. Seeing new places. Experiencing new things. And re-living old places and events, but with the new insight that being with you brings. As I look at these pictures, almost twenty years later, that hasn't changed. There is no place I'd rather be than with you.

Us

paper travel souvenirs

I'd be the first to agree that it is much more fun to scrapbook new, clear, crisp pictures. But the memories represented with older, less clear photos are equally important and deserve to be saved. Adding memorabilia, here in a torn vellum pocket, spreads out the emphasis so the only focus isn't on the less-than-stellar photos.

WE IS ALWAYS BETTER THAN I
Supplies: Patterned papers (Chatterbox); label holder (Karen Foster Design); tag (Making Memories); twill (May Arts); brads (ScrapArts); vellum (Close To My Heart); jump ring (Darice); stamp (Office Depot); stamping ink

A day with the mouse. You know what I remember most about the day? The way you smiled when the rotten child who was teasing the goat got butted on her hind end by that same goat as soon as she turned her back to it. This was one of the very special days for your surprise birthday weekend. A weekend I will never forget.

She's 9, and supposed to love shopping. NOT. Olivia would rather do anything (even clean her room) than shop. She likes to complain about not having enough clothes or the right shoes, but she sure doesn't want to go out and purchase them herself. I love to shop. Is this my kid?

CHOOSE JUICY

JUICY COUTURE

www.juicycouture.com

This is a one of a kind restyled vintage garment. The denim is intended to fray and fringe. Feel free to trim after washing. Enjoy your Firefly Vintage!

FASHION

embellishments

Most scrapbookers love embellishments and are constantly searching for a page accent that is just right for whatever layouts they are working on. It is easy to forget that memorabilia items make some of the best page accents. Not only are the items already on hand, they are sure to bring new meaning to your photos and stories because they are relevant and related.

Embellishments can be placed directly on the layout, on top of journaling boxes, over or next to photos, on metal frames and on tags. In fact, memorabilia-type embellishments can go anywhere or on anything included on your page. The best method of attaching the memorabilia depends completely on what type of item it is.

Whatever you are saving, experiment with different types of memorabilia for one-of-a-kind page embellishments.

Memorabilia for page embellishments

Some memorabilia items that make fantastic page embellishments are:

- Awards
- Bookmarks or book pages
- Buttons and pins
- CDs and disks
- Coins
- Doll or baby clothes
- Dried, pressed flowers and leaves

- Event tags
- Fabric and lace
- Flat rocks
- Game pieces and cards
- Gift cards
- Hair holders and accents
- Jewelry and watches

- Labels from clothes, food, toys, appliances
- Mass cards
- Matchbooks
- Notes and letters
- Recipes
- Small toys

EXTREME makeover, girls BEDROOM ediTion

A & J

A &

remodeling remnants

Remodeling the girls' room was a huge chore, as they could not agree on a color scheme or overall concept. Working for a successful resolution was not nearly as easy as it should have been. However, once I found a hair bow in colors both girls liked, and paint they could agree on, the rest fell into place. The paint chip used to determine wall color and scraps of the ribbons used to hang pictures from the wall are fun reminders of what we went through to get the look they wanted.

EXTREME MAKEOVER...
Supplies: Patterned papers (KI Memories, Paper Fever); die-cut letters (QuickKutz); eyelets (Making Memories); ribbon (May Arts); cardstock; paint chip; transparency

The only significant problem with our new house (other than the 70's fixtures) was the size of the kids' bedrooms. They are way too small! Our first major project was the girls' room. Amy really wanted to keep her queen sized bed, and Joani really didn't want to continue sleeping on her mattress on the floor. Because the Tommy Hilfiger bedding was so spendy that became the girls' birthday gifts and the rest of the makeover was on us. I pulled out the cedar closet boards, painted the closets and inserted organizers before we moved in, so all that was left was painting two walls Fuschia Fizz (Amy wanted pink and purple, Joani wanted orange and blue...OY!), buying the needed accessories, building the loft and getting it done. The project took a full week, but the end result was well worth it. The girls love their room, it is clean, has room to move and is clutter free, and Brian even likes it!

2004

...and you couldn't be prouder! Chalk this up to another one of Chandler's and my "girly" influences on your life. Your dad would have liked for you to be 10 or 11 before getting your ears pierced ... but the three of us convinced him that seven is the perfect age. Girl power ... oh yeah!

shopping bag

Not only does the bag from an ear-piercing event make a cute accent, it acts as a great title. This quick and simple layout shines because of the blend of the elements and use of memorabilia (the cute photo of Sarah is just a bonus).

JUST GOT MY EARS PIERCED, Shelley Laming
Supplies: Ribbon (May Arts); shopping bag; cardstock; pen

clothing tags

The tags from her favorite brands of clothing are sure to make Sydney smile in later years as she looks back at this glimpse of her preferences at age 9. Diana does a wonderful job of allowing the sweet nature of her little girl shine on this page.

LOVE YOUR STYLE, Diana Hudson
Supplies: Patterned papers (Karen Foster Design, KI Memories); letter stickers (American Crafts, Carolee's Creations); chipboard flowers, brads (Making Memories); cardstock

TIP As an alternative to stitching, wet glue—such as Tombow's Mono Multi—is great for adhering many types of fabric and small paper items. It offers a strong hold, it dries clear and spills can be removed when dry with a rubber cement adhesive pick-up eraser.

wedding invitations

The wording chosen to invite guests to a wedding goes a long way in setting the tone and mood of the wedding and it tells a little bit about both the bride and the groom. This one does such a nice job of summarizing the event that it seemed a shame not to utilize it on the page. By cutting the invitation in half, both the pretty front and the informative inside can be seen and enjoyed at a glance.

SHAWN & KIM
Supplies: Embossed paper, brads (K & Company); ribbon (Offray); charm (Jest Charming); stamping ink; cardstock

souvenir pins

Layout inspiration can be found everywhere, in common as well as unusual things. The idea for this page came from a quilted wall hanging my mom made to store the many pins she has saved. Among the mementos she purchased during an Alaskan cruise were pins from several of the places they visited. I used wire cutters to remove the pin backs and adhered each one with a heavy-duty Sticky Dot.

ALASKAN CRUISE
Supplies: Die-cut letters (QuicKutz); ink (Close To My Heart)

mitten clips

The mitten clips used to hold Toria's mittens to her coat make a great reminder of the fun she had while playing in the snow. As she outgrows the need for mitten clips, she will forever be able to look back and remember how useful they once were. They also add a soft sentiment to the page, and Denise will get as much joy from seeing this childhood reminder as will Toria.

SNOW, Denise Tucker
Supplies: Patterned papers (Basic Grey, EK Success); vellum (Paper Palette); metal letters (EK Success); molding strip, flower brads (Making Memories); metal charms (Boutique Trims); stamps (All Night Media); fiber (Fibers By The Yard); silver leafing pen (Krylon); stamping ink; acrylic paint; foam adhesive; mitten clips

TIP Flat but oddly shaped items—such as these mitten clips—might best be adhered with mounting foam or Pop Dots on the back, adhesives that raise and even out the surface being adhered to paper for better, firmer hold.

medals

In hindsight all those medals are a bit heavy for one page, but the convenience of having them all in one place, with the photos and story they represent, is nice. By gluing three sheets of cardstock together, I was able to make a base that supports the bulk of the weight caused by the medals. An added bonus to using medals on a page like this is that they detract from the poor quality of the old photos. They simply work well with the story and assorted pictures to offer a complete look at that element of my childhood.

ALL THAT REMAINS

Supplies: Ribbon (May Arts); transparency; cardstock

TIP Heavy items, such as jewelry or medals, work best with a very strong adhesive. Super Tape from Therm O Web is the strongest dry adhesive I have found, and it holds many things firmly in place.

After about eight years of competitive swimming I had many awards. I'd always been big for my age. I was very strong, and I was just lucky. I competed in many swim competitions and I won or placed frequently. I still remember my first trophy. It was for age group high point (most points by a swimmer in that age category) in 1973. I was so excited that I held it in my arms, looking at it, touching the metal sign, for hours. Similar joy was felt upon receiving the first medal, ribbon and plaque. After a while receiving the awards wasn't as exciting or special any more. The joy I'd felt with competition was gone. The commitment swimming had become was too big. It took too much time each day and involved most weekends as well. I wanted to try other sports. I wanted to do sleepovers with friends from school. I wanted something different. After I quit swimming I wanted to get rid of all my awards. They were dust collectors and something that was no longer a part of my life. Instead, I took them down off my shelves and boxed them up. Over the years more and more got tossed with each move. Now, these few medals are all that remain. And I'm good with that.

CORI J. MARCHER

school artwork

Scanning and reducing artwork is one of many creative and effective ways to save it in an album. By reducing the size of the finished pieces, Pam is able to include several in a small amount of space. Combined with pictures taken during the year the art was created, this layout saves many memories in a neat and concise way.

KINDERGARTEN, Pam Kopka

Supplies: Patterned papers, sticker, twill (Scenic Route Paper Co.); brads (Provo Craft); flowers, spiral paper clip, ribbon (Making Memories); epoxy accents (EK Success); cork paper (Duck Products)

yugioh

A handful of cards

Ultra, ultimate & super rare

Spell, magic, masters, trap & common cards

5 pieces of Exodia

Trading and battling with friends

Promo rare & holofoil

magic

The good life

collector cards

Those shiny little cards hold a magnetic appeal for my youngest son. Collecting and trading them was of primary importance during his 4th-grade year, so I thought he'd like it if I included some of them on a layout. After he got over the shock of seeing his beloved cards forever ruined by having thread run through them, he laughed and smiled as he realized they were cards from Mom's stack that had been defaced. Years down the road, when the cards are faded or long gone, he'll have this photo, this story, this glimpse of what really mattered in the 4th grade.

YU-GI-OH MAGIC
Supplies: Die-cut letters (QuicKutz); ribbon (May Arts, SEI); cardstock; stamping ink

TIP Keep in mind that any wet adhesive will cause some degree of warping on paper items—even thicker paper such as these collector cards. Larger items made of paper are best anchored with dry adhesive or with stitching.

cherish

all that is dear

envelopes & enclosures

Envelopes and enclosures rank right up there with pockets and pouches in terms of ease of use, availability and affordability.

For safety reasons, for privacy issues, or for ease or convenience, sometimes things just need to be tucked into an envelope or a secured enclosure. Memorabilia does not have to be readily visible to be saved and enjoyed. Putting a private letter or document on the back of a layout in an envelope that can be opened is a perfectly acceptable way to save an item.

You can make envelopes by tracing templates and cutting out the traced shapes. They can be customized to fit anything. They are easily cut apart, sanded, stained, embossed or layered. They can even act as a base for a page.

Usually made from paper or vellum, envelopes and enclosures can also be made from plastic and fabric. Be creative in your choice of materials to create the perfect hiding place for your personal treasures.

Everyday memorabilia

Small, flat souvenirs and keepsakes are easily tucked into little envelopes and enclosures, while documents and news clippings are safely preserved in larger envelopes and enclosures. Here are some ideas for treasures that work well in envelopes and enclosures:

- Bookmarks
- Buttons
- Coins
- Hardware
- Jewelry

- Keys
- Musical paraphernalia
- Newspaper clippings
- Personal notes and letters
- Pressed flowers

- Religious mementos
- Swatches
- Tags
- Toys
- Trinkets

musical paraphernalia

The envelope-enclosed picks are perfect for this layout of Ryan playing the guitar. But the story Diana tells adds even more to the page. The picks aren't just representative of Ryan's latest love...they are the items she currently finds in his pockets when doing laundry. She acknowledges the place those picks have in his present and future, while admitting that she misses the tiny toys she found in his pockets in the past. To make the picks really stand out against the background paper, she added a scrap of patterned paper to the back of the pocket.

FUN FACT #12, Diana Hudson
Supplies: Patterned papers (Autumn Leaves, Paper Loft); cloth tag reinforcements (7 Gypsies); string closure (Karen Foster Design); alphabet tabs (Autumn Leaves); distress ink (Ranger); number stamps (Making Memories); staples

collectible items

There are many details I don't know about my maternal grandparents. I've several vague memories of stories I've heard yet only pieces of those stories remain in my memory banks. Little gaps of missing information leave me frustrated when trying to recall specific details. For this layout, rather than focusing on many of the things I can't quite remember, I shared a few recollections about things I remember clearly: childhood visits to their home and playing with some of the items they collected. Using a few pieces from their collections—such as a lace doily in a translucent vellum envelope and coins in a PVC-free plastic envelope—reinforces the sentiment behind the shared story.

LITTLE TREASURES

Supplies: Patterned papers (My Minds Eye); die-cut letters (QuicKutz); dimensional adhesive (JudiKins); vellum envelope (DMD); plastic envelope (3M); distress ink (Ranger); ribbon (Offray); cardstock

TIP By owning just a few envelope and shape templates, you can make a huge variety of envelopes in whatever color and style you like. Add an inch or two to either height or width to create a custom envelope in no time at all.

friendship bracelet

My oldest daughter has some fabulous friends— girls who are sweet and smart and special. Julia is one of them. For the journaling on this page I listed a few of the things both girls have in common or enjoy doing together. The story of the yellow bracelet is told on the back of the page, and that is a link they continue to share (only this year the bracelet is black).

FRIENDS

Supplies: Patterned papers (Mustard Moon); metal letters (Colorbök); plastic envelope (Therm O Web); ribbon (May Arts); brads (ScrapArts); stamping ink

letter to a newborn

Some documents are too personal or private for the general public to view, yet they are important to us and we want to save them. Envelopes and enclosures are the best storage option for such memorabilia. Diana tucked her heartfelt journaling into the envelope she used as a portion of the base for this newborn photo. Individual stickers, randomly laid out as a large photo mat, add to the sentimental feel. Though Diana used the envelope to save her feelings about her daughter, and the relationship they share, many types of memorabilia can be included. The envelope would make a handy place to store a copy of her birth certificate, hospital bracelet or newborn hand- and footprints.

HEAVEN SENT, Diana Hudson

Supplies: Stickers (Pebbles); rub-on words (Making Memories); twill ribbon (Scenic Route Paper Co.); postage stamp charm (Foofala); "s" monogram (Mustard Moon); envelope template (Deluxe Designs); eyelets (Creative Imaginations); cardstock

cherished toys

A little girl's treasures are important and special pieces of childhood. The large stuffed lamb may not have survived a house with three older boys, but Toria will always have a small, soft section of its tail to rub and remember how soft the lamb was. Denise glued the torn tail to a piece of cardstock and tucked it, with its story, in a vellum envelope. By mounting sections of patterned paper with foam, as well as the matted photos, Denise has created an entire page of dimension, keeping the height evenly distributed between the fluffy envelope and the other page elements.

PRETTY IN PINK, Denise Tucker

Supplies: Patterned papers, rub-on letters (Rusty Pickle); vellum (Paper Palette); metal corners, charm (Making Memories); buckle, button (Junkitz); label holder (KI Memories); ribbon (Offray, Stampendous!); letter stamps (All Night Media); heart stamp (Prickley Pear Rubber Stamps); distress ink, UTEE (Ranger); cardstock; acrylic paint; stamping ink; netting

 TIP Sometimes special items clash with the photos that go with them. Keeping the memorabilia with its story and photos ensures that they are always available, regardless if included on the front or the back of a page. If you wish to include the items on the front of a page as shown below, a translucent vellum envelope will help diffuse the look off the contents.

heritage wedding keepsakes

Both of my husband's parents have passed away. Sadly neither I, nor the kids, had a chance to meet Brian's mom, though we were all blessed for many years by knowing Papa Gary. These photos from their wedding, along with all the newspaper clippings, flight stubs and their wedding certificate, help the kids learn a little about the grand-mother they never knew, as well as see a different side of the grandfather they knew and loved. The large vellum en-velope is perfect for storing the assortment of items they'd saved from their special day, and the mini flip book allowed me to include the best of the photos in one place.

NEWLYWEDS

Supplies: Patterned papers (My Minds Eye); metal hat pins (EK Success); die-cut heart (Deluxe Designs); flowers, safety pin (Making Memories); vellum envelope (Paper Source); charm, brads (ScrapArts); ribbon (Offray); cardstock; stamping ink

SMILE TO REMEMBER

When the dentist mentioned that it was necessary for you to wear an apparatus to correct your cross-bite, I thought you might be apprehensive. You were a little trooper though. You allowed the dentist and his assistant to insert the bit of metal, and you wore it without complaint for 8 months. We returned every 6 weeks for a check and fitting (sometimes tightening was necessary). You never cried or fussed...even when you couldn't chew gum with the other kids. We made sure to keep sugarless on hand as much as possible. The result was beautiful! I love to see you smile! Summer, 2005

dental appliances

Such a beautiful smile on such a darling little girl. Angelia shares the story of what a good sport Michaela was during the ordeal of wearing a mouth appliance to help correct a cross bite. Michaela was so young when she wore the metal mouthpiece that she probably won't remember the experience. Since Angelia saved the mouthpiece, Michaela can look at this page later in life and see one of the reasons why she has such a beautiful smile. Using a sturdy, PVC-free plastic envelope will help prevent the metal from poking through the plastic over time.

SMILE TO REMEMBER, Angelia Wigginton
Supplies: Patterned papers (KI Memories; Scrapworks), letter stickers (Scrapworks); rickrack (Doodlebug Design); rub-on letters (K & Company); ribbon (May Arts, Offray); photo corners (Canson); cardstock

product labels

While attending a scrapbook getaway with some folks from work, I saw these photos sitting in front of Armida. She was smiling as she was pondering how to best save these darling snapshots. I knew immediately which papers would be a perfect match, and I practically begged her to allow me to scrap them for her. She graciously agreed, and I had a blast working with such inspiring photos. That adorable little girl is an imp, and it clearly shows in her effort to get to the chocolate. Success is sweet, and the quickly discarded Hershey's syrup wrapper included on the layout shows that the term "safety seal" can not deter a determined 2-year-old.

SWEET SATISFACTION

*Photos: Armida Nunez-Finley, Ridgefield, Washington
Supplies: Patterned papers, ribbon (SEI); chipboard letter (Making Memories); plastic envelope (Karen Foster Design); letter stickers (American Crafts); wood letters (Westrim); eyelet (Doodlebug Design); cardstock; acrylic paint; stamping ink*

sweet SATISFACTION

A pantry door and a security wrapper are no match for a determined little girl.

Remillong cell...title-clinching win

TROJANS 35

TROJANS 35

CR8WE

Trojans take the title

TROJANS 35

With David John leading the way our Trojan team took county title my senior year. Cheering for the school team is a blast no matter what, but when the team goes to Division finals the ride is incredibly exciting. I saved some of the many photos taken by our local paper, the Argus Courier, of our team and specifically David John, on its rise to the top.

DJ
David John

Just thinking about him makes me smile. In 1981 he moved to Petaluma from San Francisco and lived around the corner, on Elm St, with the Bond family. My mom and Beverly taught together and introduced us. We were friends from the first, though I think it was more him wanting a ride to school than anything else. He played basketball and I was a cheerleader so our hours were similar and we spent a lot of time together, much to the chagrin of one of his girlfriends. He was the first guy I could just hang out and be with. I helped him become a little more conscientious about school work, he helped me not take it all so seriously.

We kept in touch for a few years after high school and then time and distance became a factor. I still think of him every once in a while and I'm grateful that I had the chance to know him and to call him "friend".

newspaper clippings

My preppy, GQ buddy from high school sure kept the sports writers at the Argus Courier on their toes. No album including my memories from Petaluma High would be complete without including David John Miles. As a cheerleader I attended every basketball game and clipped every photo from our local paper of David. Storing all those clippings in one clear pouch allows me to save them as well as enjoy their content. When paired with his senior picture and the story of our friendship, the memory is permanently saved in one location.

DAVID JOHN
Supplies: Patterned paper (Keeping Memories Alive); ribbon (May Arts, SEI); eyelets (Making Memories); transparency, plastic pocket (Office Depot); stamping ink; cardstock

Trojans take the title

mass cards

My husband's maternal grandparents overcame incredible odds and succeeded. Though I never had the chance to meet them, the newspaper clippings my mother-in-law saved allows our family to see just a bit of who they were. Their mass cards alone tell something about them. In addition to their names, dates and locations of birth and death and place of internment they tell of their Catholic faith and commitment. The articles written about them and a few of their experiences are included in the envelope, telling us a bit more about some of the struggles they faced in a new country. By simply tearing and inking an old envelope, I was able to tuck in numerous bits of their lives.

THEIR STORY

Supplies: Patterned papers, stickers (K & Company); label holder (Daisy D's); letter sticker (EK Success); tag (Making Memories); letter stamps (PSX Design); brads (ScrapArts); ribbon (Offray); cardstock; stamping ink; lace; old buttons; doily

sorority bids

My mom joined a sorority in college. Many years later, so did I. My grandmother never had that chance, yet she made sure that both my mom and I did. After my grandfather passed away, when Grama was getting ready to move, we found an old envelope—which I adhered with dry adhesive and adorned with a ribbon border—full of the sorority bids my mom had received almost 40 years earlier. They were so important to my grandmother that she'd saved them all that time. Those saved bids help share my grandmother's story, and they offer testimony to her personality. Additional instructions are on page 92.

KYLA

Supplies: Patterned paper (K & Company); envelope (DMD); solvent ink (Tsukineko); brads (ScrapArts); ribbon, letters (Making Memories); stickers (Magenta)

HOW TO MAKE A ZIPPERED ENCLOSURE

know HOW

1 Choose a zipper in a color and size to match your layout needs. Cut a piece of paper to fit either just inside or just outside of the zip area. Cut the paper to make the enclosure into two sections, one for each edge of the zipper. Place a strip of ⅛" Super Tape on either the underside of both sections of paper or right next to the teeth on both sides of the top of the zipper. Zippers are slippery and you will save yourself frustration if you secure the paper to the zipper before sewing.

2 Use a sewing machine or needle and thread to sew the paper to the zipper. Then adhere the rest of your enclosure to your layout in any manner you like. Note: Don't sew through the Super Tape. It will gum up your needle, tear your paper and possibly jam your machine. That is why the tape goes so close to the teeth, so there is room to sew the paper to the zipper without having to sew through the adhesive. If you sew by hand, poke your holes in the paper before sewing to make the task quicker and the stitch length even, and you will have advance warning if you get too close to the tape.

personal notes

My youngest daughter was none too pleased when we decided to move from the West Side to Vancouver. She made that abundantly clear. After we moved and my husband set up the backup computer in our room, he found some notes she'd written about her displeasure. Her drama queen nature shone through as she shared how her life was over. Rotten parents that we are, we both smiled and laughed. By that time she'd already made several new friends and was happy with the move. This picture, taken almost one year to the day later, shows how happy she is and how well she's adjusted. Wanting her to be able to look back and see how she felt, yet not wanting those private thoughts shared with anyone who sees her albums, I made a zippered enclosure to store them. She can look back, read and share those notes as she chooses. To make the clear plastic heart stand out more, I inked the heart (because plastic doesn't soak up the ink, either dye or pigment-based ink can be used) and embossed it with clear embossing powder. The heart, while remaining translucent, took on a hint of the color of ink that was used.

JONES
Supplies: Patterned papers (Basic Grey); letter stickers (K & Company); die-cut letters (QuicKutz); ribbon (May Arts); brad (Doodlebug Design); heart (Heidi Swapp); stamping ink; zipper

shakers
& frames

Perfect for minute items or memorabilia that really needs to stand out and be showcased, a shaker or a frame can be the ideal setting for tiny treasures.

All frames that can be used in a scrapbook album can be made into shakers. However, a shaker doesn't necessarily have to be made from a frame. The main difference is that a shaker holds an item that moves or has the ability to move within a controlled setting, while a frame houses a non-movable item.

Small or finely detailed items can get lost within a busy pattern on a scrapbook page. By surrounding the item with a frame, you help draw attention to the item by grounding it with visual weight. Larger items can also benefit from the presence of a frame because a frame says, "I am important." When you want a particular treasure to take center stage, placing it within a notable frame is a surefire way to make a statement.

HOW TO MAKE A SHAKER FRAME

1 Use Super Tape to adhere a piece of transparency film to the backside of your foam-core frame to create the window. If you are going to cover the front of the frame in patterned paper, stamp on it or add words or color, do that before securing the transparency.

2 Use Pop Dots or foam mounting tape to create depth. If needed, use additional layers of foam mounting tape, one on top of another, to achieve the needed depth. If you don't want the memorabilia item to move within the frame, be sure to add tacky tape to the back of the item prior to enclosing it.

3 Place items loosely or secure them within the window and peel off tape to secure backing. Use additional tacky tape to hold shaker in place on your page.

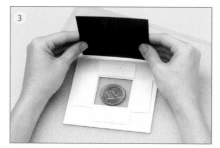

There goes my boy, off into the mountains with everything he will need for the weekend carried on his back. We had already bought lots of new gear for Boy Scouts, but we needed to buy more new equipment for backpacking. When you are carrying everything, weight becomes very important. We got the lighter-weight sleeping bag, a new backpacking tent, and even a lighter flashlight for Eric. This day was actually a practice run for Eric to get used to his back before setting off with the Troop. Eric really enjoys backpacking and the sense of peace that comes from treading where few people venture.

map scraps

Mat board frames make fantastic shakers, as do slide mounts. These two items also make excellent frames for items that don't need to move or shake. Kelli takes such extraordinary photos that her enlargements almost come to life. A little weariness and a whole lot of determination are clearly seen in this backpack view of her son. Using a section of map to create the frame adds visual interest, and the addition of the compass reinforces the overall theme.

EXPLORER, Kelli Noto

Supplies: Map (Rand McNally); die-cut letters (QuickKutz); dimensional adhesive (JudiKins); ribbon (Carolee's Creations); mounting foam (3M); compass (Target); cardstock; chipboard

TIP Frames are readily available in a variety of sizes and come in card-stock weight, plastic, metal, wood and acrylic. By covering the front and back with window plastic (transparency) or vellum you can neatly house a variety of items.

glass shards

When a fire destroyed the church Elizabeth and her family attend, she chose to look at the positive. She saved a few important pieces of her old church to help her family remember what once was. Because the broken stained-glass pieces can be dangerous, she affixed them inside metal frames and softened their sharp edges by covering them in diamond glaze. The glaze dries clear, allowing the rich color of the stained glass to shine through. The glaze also hardens as it dries and holds the jagged pieces firmly and safely in place. The intermittent placement, combined with heartfelt journaling and touching photos, adds power to her statement that the flames were not able to destroy the heart of the church. Additional instructions are on page 92.

THE FLAMES SHALL NOT HURT THEE, Elizabeth Ruuska

Supplies: Patterned papers, fabric swatch (Junkitz); frames, brads, flowers (Making Memories); sticky strips (Therm O Web); alcohol inks (Ranger); dimensional adhesive (JudiKins)

TIP Shakers are particularly effective for showcasing small particles such as rice, confetti, dried seeds or leaves, sand and beads.

'04

We went to three different pumpkin patches this year. The dragon patch, a fun patch with huge bulls, a hay maze and tire swing, and a new farm that was built by a computer genius who is also a midget. It had a full, kids sized mining town, a pirate ship and your favorite, a Swiss Family Robinson style tree house. He was building a castle, complete with draw bridge and moat, while we were there. I can't imagine a time when you are too old to enjoy all the fun that fall brings.

seeds

After seeing a demonstration that showed how sunflower seeds are removed from the flowers, salted and dried, my kids became temporarily addicted to them. Though I didn't take pictures of the actual demonstration, the kids did save some of the seeds used. Combining those seeds—sandwiched between die-cut letter frames that are fashioned into shaker boxes with transparency film and foam spacers—with photos taken during the same event tie together both memories and make a fun page accent.

FALL FUN

Supplies: Patterned papers (Chatterbox); letter stickers (American Crafts); number stickers (KI Memories); die-cut letter frames (Deluxe Designs); transparency (Office Depot); mounting foam (3M); cardstock

souvenir postcards, pressed coins

The bright colors seen at M&M World and on the postcard are toned down beautifully by the use of paper in the same, yet slightly softer, shades. Diana does such a great job incorporating her memorabilia into the body of her layout that I had to remind myself that it was there! Carrying the circle theme throughout the page keeps the viewer's eyes moving, and the square and rectangle elements are a perfect counter balance. The vellum on top of the postcard is not only a great way to save the message found on the back of the postcard, it also tones down the bright color and doesn't allow the postcard to detract from the main photos. Using image-editing software to change Sydney to black-and-white was sheer genius. In a page infused with bold color, her daughter shines due to the absence of color.

M&M'S WORLD, Diana Hudson
Supplies: Patterned papers (SEI); poem stones, mini brads (Creative Imaginations); tag (American Tag Co.); circle template (Provo Craft); circle punches (EK Success, Marvy); cardstock; acrylic paint; vellum

Sydney could not resist turning a penny into a souvenir from M&Ms World. She had looked forward to this stop during our trip for weeks!

April 15, 2003
Daddy,
We're having a great time. Wish you were here!
Love,
Sydney

I loved everything about my senior year. I had the chance to cheer for both football and basketball. Our squad got along really well. We had a blast at cheer camp. I was able to swim for the school team. I received a student-of-the-month award and scholarship. I was accepted at all the colleges I applied to. I was a counselor for 6th grade outdoor school and had way too much fun. Our trip to D-land was incredible. The prom was special and all that a prom should be. And for the first time ever I actually enjoyed getting my picture taken. I only wish everyone could experience a senior year like I had.

class of '83

TIP Frames tend to make excellent shakers because a portion of the work is already done for you. The center is already absent, saving you a step in the creation process.

preserved petals

The dried petals of a rose given by a dear friend and my diploma all work together to share the memory of the fun I had during my senior year of high school. I freely admit that I hate getting my picture taken. It's probably the main reason I'm usually the one behind the camera. Yet the photographer who took my senior pictures did a great job of putting me at ease and made the experience almost enjoyable.

CLASS OF '83
Photos: Robert Pierce Studios, Santa Rosa, California
Supplies: Patterned papers (Kopp Design); die-cut letters (QuicKutz); metal frame (Scrapworks); word tag (Target); ribbon (May Arts, Offray, Scenic Route Paper Co.); photo corners (Canson); eyelets (ScrapArts); mounting foam (3M); cardstock; acrylic paint

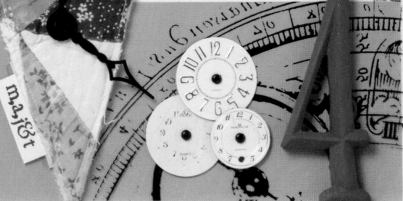

Treasures. Little pieces of life that make us smile, or laugh or cry. The heart is cut from the quilt dad & I had on our bed for 15 years. The watch faces are from Great Grama's, Papa Gary's and Grandma Carol's watches. The four symbolizes the four of you. Each item on here is special and treasured, just like each of you.

LOVE

majet

dimensional showcases

CHAPTER SEVEN

Originally used by graphic artists and architects, foam core has worked its way into craft rooms around the world. Generally composed of a polystyrene center sandwiched between two facings or "skins" of cardstock or craft paper, this lightweight material adds dimension to any scrapbook memorabilia project.

One of the main benefits of using foam core is the built-in depth. Bulky, sharp and odd-shaped items can be safely and beautifully displayed in your albums. Storing the items in a page or frame made from foam core not only helps protect the item itself, but it helps protect the other pages in the album from being bent or damaged due to the inclusion of bulky memorabilia.

I hope these pages inspire you to look at your saved memorabilia with a new eye, allowing you insight into ways three-dimensional family treasures can still be included with the photos and stories that make them so very special.

HOW TO USE FOAM CORE

Foam core is a fantastic option for showcasing many bulky items because it fits beautifully in most albums, is easy to access and is fairly inexpensive. Best of all, it is photo-friendly and painless to use. I've found it at office supply and super stores, in both black and white, but it's also available in other colors at art supply stores. Two items that help ensure that your foam core project will be successful are a sharp craft knife (or blade-type cutter) and a clear ruler. A sharp, fresh blade means a clean, even cut on the foam. A clear ruler allows you to see exactly where you need to cut. Both will not only simplify the process, they will make it a whole lot more fun.

If you are planning to embellish the paper that will lie over the foam core, I highly recommend doing that prior to adhering it to the foam core. Foam core is dense but fairly soft, and any amount of pushing will affect the surface of the foam core.

1 Use the clear ruler to measure and mark the area that will be cut. The sample and layouts have been done with the openings in square and rectangle shapes, but circles and ovals can be made as well. Due to their straight lines, squares and rectangles are easier to cut. With a cutting mat in place beneath your project, cut out the unneeded area of foam with a craft knife.

2 Once the section has been removed, cover the front of the project with selected paper. Book binding adhesive, double-sided tape and Mod Podge all work well for secure coverage. If using a wet adhesive, make sure it is completely dry before cutting out the paper that covers the opening in the foam core.

3 Cut out the paper that covers the created opening in the foam core. You can make the cut exact by using a craft knife right next to the edge of the foam core, or you can lightly sand the excess paper away with a nail file or sandpaper. Use the same method to trim around the edges of the page or frame.

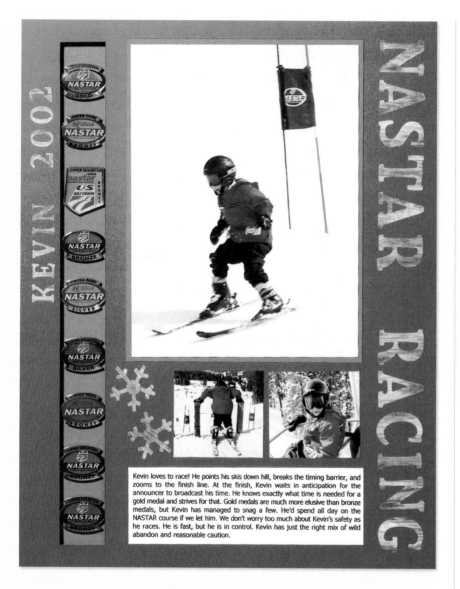

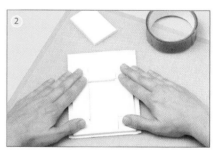

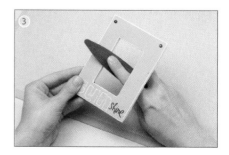

award pins

Memorabilia aspect aside, those award pins make an exceptionally eye-catching page accent. They are neatly and safely stored with the photos that tell their story. By snipping off the pin backs with wire snips, Kelli was able to save the season of memories on one effective page.

NASTAR, Kelli Noto

Supplies: Die-cut letters, shapes (QuicKutz); acrylic paint; cardstock; transparency; pins; foam core

fishing lures

Peaceful, serene and tranquil; the quiet solitude shown in these photos is reflected by the calm water, the still grass and the peaceful look on Eric's face. The color over black-and-white technique Kelli used to accentuate the photos and memories is beautifully balanced by the colors found in the lures she mounted. Someday a different type of fly may be used for fishing, but Eric will always be able to recall ones from his childhood.

FISHING, Kelli Noto

Supplies: Letter templates (Deja Views); die-cut letters (QuickKutz); fishing lures; foam core; cardstock

TIP White seems to be the most common color of foam core, but black is also available and makes a beautiful choice for many projects. Try covering the foam core with patterned paper to match your page theme with ease!

pet keepsakes

My first dog, or at least the first I remember having, was a friend beyond compare...a faithful and forever friend. I won't ever forget him or the role he played in my life, and my children are now able to see and share that story with me. His dog tags are long gone, but the little black collar he wore as a puppy reminds me of what a wonderful little lap dog he was.

FAITHFUL FRIEND

Supplies: Patterned papers (My Minds Eye); buttons (7 Gypsies); word stickers (S.R.M. Press); letter stickers (Scrapworks); embroidery floss; cardstock; foam core

TIP Standard foam core thicknesses are ⅛" to ³/₁₆". By trimming the desired piece to ¼" smaller than your page, it can be placed in most brands of page protectors.

award ribbons

Ribbons, especially ribbons with big rosettes, can be tough to save. Sometimes it is easier to take a picture of the ribbon than it is to include it on a page or in an album. But other times saving the actual award itself is important to the person who earned it. That was the case here. Matt worked very hard for his ribbon and plaque, and he wanted me to save them. Foam core allowed me to even out the surface a bit. While still a little bumpy and lumpy, it is smooth enough to not damage the pages that come before and after it in his album.

DONE IN ONE YEAR

Supplies: Patterned paper (Imagination Project); letter stickers (Doodlebug Design); poem stones (Creative Imaginations); date stamp, transparency (Office Depot); tag (Making Memories); brads (ScrapArts); stamping ink; foam core

show souvenirs

What a lucky young man Trent is! A trip to NYC with his high-school band not only allowed him an opportunity to see the city, it allowed him a chance to see a live Broadway play. It is a trip I'm sure he will never forget, and Denise's use of the program—held in place in a page-size frame with elastic bands—ticket stub and key chain will allow him to share his treasured memories with his future spouse and children. If you find your ticket stubs wrinkled from improper storage, do not try to iron them. As a built-in security measure, heat causes these ticket stubs to turn black. A second frame, circle cut into the foam-core page, provides a fun showcase for dangling a keychain souvenir.

WICKED PLAYBILL, Denise Tucker

Supplies: Patterned paper (Basic Grey); foam paper (Flora-Craft); vellum (Paper Palette); brads (Creative Impressions); ribbon (Making Memories); specialty paint (Krylon); stamping ink; foam adhesive; embossing powder; key chain; theater stub; playbill; washers; elastic

TIM ♥ 1997

Before the days of Eeyore you loved a bear named **POOH**. He was your first friend. He was your favorite friend. He is a forever friend. The pooh (and Eeyore) **MOVIES**

TIP While early foam core was highly acidic and decomposed fairly quickly, there are many foam core lines currently on the market for archival use. In fact, it is a staple for framing archival artwork.

clothing remnants

Articles of clothing, or trimmed down sections of old clothes, can be made into page accents full of meaning and sentiment. I can't count the number of times I picked up that Pooh shirt off the floor and re-dressed that bear—which is preserved in a tiny spiral album mounted in a foam core page. The item was meaningful to a little boy who matters a whole lot to me. Tim can see what was important to him as a toddler, and I have a visual reminder of how much a little boy loved his bear.

THE POOH BEAR STORY

Supplies: Patterned paper (Basic Grey); spiral book (DMD); letter stickers (American Crafts); label maker (Dymo); epoxy stickers (EK Success); plastic envelope (Therm O Web); ribbon (May Arts, Offray); brads (ScrapArts); letter stamps (PSX Design); die-cut photo turns (QuicKutz); pen; stamping ink; foam core

I can't even begin to count the number of eye glasses you've "borrowed" from various family members. Usually you just wore them for a bit and then put them down in a place known only to you. Sometimes they'd turn up weeks later; in a boot in the bottom of the closet, inside a closed Tupperware container in the pantry, once we found a pair in the butter dish. We all learned quickly; NO GLASSES FOR JOAN!! It's a dang good thing you are so stinking cute.

TIP Foam core (or Foamcore, depending on the brand and manufacturer) is found at art supply shops, office supply stores and at most general crafts facilities. Elmer's (yes, the folks who make glue) and Monsanto are two commonly found brands, and both offer acid-free, archival-quality foam core.

eyeglasses

That little girl was so cute, she often got away with murder. Her endearing giggle, dimpled grin and good nature served her quite well. She lost many pairs of my mom's glasses. She broke a pair of my glasses and a pair of Papa Gary's. I've lost count of the number of sunglasses that disappeared or broke due to her tiny hands. Saving that story, with one of her glasses victims, will remind her to take a deep breath should any of her children be inclined to follow in her footsteps. After all, I'm told history repeats itself.

GLASSES THIEF
Supplies: Patterned papers (KI Memories, Paper Fever); rub-on letters (Scrapworks); letter stickers (American Crafts); die-cut tag topper (QuicKutz); ribbon (May Arts); cardstock; foam core

playtime trinkets

While these pictures crack me up, they make my husband cringe; as he doesn't have any sisters, the way little girls play was a continual surprise to him. Fortunately, if Tim ever has a daughter, he will already be well-versed in the ways of little girls. The saved pieces of beads and old makeup act as a silly reminder that boys and girls don't have to play differently to have fun.

WHEN YOU HAVE BIG SISTERS
Supplies: Patterned papers, cardstock letters (Basic Grey); letter stickers (Chatterbox); date stamp (Office Depot); cardstock; stamping ink; old makeup; beads; foam core

military documents

My father-in-law was a wonderful and funny man. He could talk and talk and talk. But when we'd ask him about certain things, like his time in England during the second World War, he was very closed-mouthed. When he gave me these pictures, I asked him about them, but he just changed the subject. After he passed away, his discharge papers were in a box we received and we learned a little more about his time in Europe. The discharge papers—housed and protected in a foam core frame that is cut the entire size of the page— along with his Social Security card and some hospital documents were found in this leather folder. A shaker box made from patterned paper and transparency film handily holds vintage-era coins.

WW2

Supplies: Patterned papers (KI Memories, Rusty Pickle); transparency, emblem (K & Company); envelope (EK Success); chipboard letters (Rusty Pickle); stamp (Me & My Big Ideas); ribbon (May Arts, Scenic Route Paper Co.); stamps (PSX Design); solvent ink (Tsukineko); brads (ScrapArts); acrylic paint; vintage coins; foam core

heritage keepsakes

This gorgeous heritage page says so much about Denise's father and his brothers. It speaks of a time many of us have only read or heard about. We can't possibly fully understand the struggle it was just to survive, because most of us haven't lived through it. Because of the story and items Denise saved, her children and their children will be able to see a small piece of an era that made or broke many people. A handmade foam core and transparency film shaker box houses vintage coins and a $2 bill.

ON THE BRINK OF 1929, Denise Tucker

Supplies: Patterned papers (Paper Loft, Rusty Pickle); embossed paper (Provo Craft); transparency (Kodak); foam core (Hunt); distress ink (Ranger); hole paper (Magic Mesh); wooden letters (Wal-Mart); acrylic letters in frames (Paper Studio); clear acrylic letters (Sulyn Industries); ribbon (Paper House); key (Rusty Pickle); label holder, brads (Making Memories); rivets (Chatterbox); corners, rub-ons (EK Success); decoupage medium (Plaid); foam adhesive; acrylic paint; embossing powder; printed word ribbon; spray adhesive; money

EAST COAST vacation

August 7-15, 1996

BOSTON

Day 1: dinner at 57 Park Plaza

Day 2: August 7, 1996 * The room @ 57 Park Plaza * Faneuil Hall

American Airlines
BOARDING PASS

MARCHER/ROBER
MILES
SAN FRANCI:
DALLAS FT W

MARCHER/ROBER
MILES
DALLAS FT W
BOSTON

MARCHER/KYLA
MILES
DALLAS FT WORTH 3E
BOSTON

AMERICAN AIRLINES
AA 192 6Z 06AUG 205P

PLEASE SEE REVERSE SIDE FOR IMPO

PLEASE REVIEW THE ENCLOS

We've already double checked them
In order to prevent any additional inc
IMMEDIATELY to Customer Serv

SALES PERSON: H9   ITINERARY
CUSTOMER NBR: 328161

TO: R MARCHER
    719 VANESSA WAY
    PETALUMA CA 94952

FOR: MARCHER/ROBERT
     MARCHER/KYL

An Invitation
Welcome to The 57

On behalf of the managem
The 57, I would like to ext
invitation to join us for lu
The 57 Restaurant to enjo
at a 15% disc

William (Billy) N. Dudaises
General Manager

putting it all
together

The first seven chapters of this book have focused on all of the special ways to treat memorabilia and the unique ways you can use memorabilia in your scrapbooks. We've looked at numerous memorabilia items across a wide array of page themes and topics. Now you're ready to put everything you've learned together into a scrapbook theme album.

As you begin gathering and sorting through your own memorabilia, you will likely see logical sets of items that go hand-in-hand with photographs from those events. Once you've gathered the memorabilia and photographs together, you'll have all that you need to join them together in theme albums that tell your own unique stories.

So gather your scrapbook supplies, keepsakes and mementos, photographs and memories and let the creativity begin. You will be richly rewarded with the most meaningful scrapbook pages yet!

baby album

Baby items are some of the easiest to save and include on scrapbook pages. Most of the items are tiny so they fit perfectly on just about any size page, and their presence adds a soft, sentimental element to completed layouts. No matter what you've chosen to save, your child, and hopefully your child's child, is sure to enjoy seeing little bits of those early days in an album.

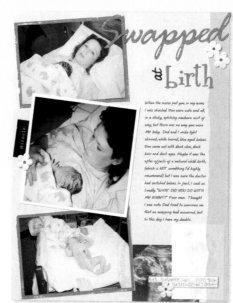

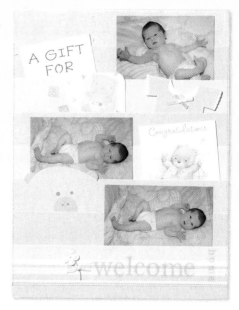

BULKIER ITEMS CAN ALSO BE PHOTO-GRAPHED, SCANNED OR COLORCOPIED

USE TINY SNIPPETS OF KEEPSAKES TO HELP TELL THE WHOLE STORY

EXPERIMENT WITH ARRANGING AND TUCKING MEMORABILIA BEHIND PHOTOS

NEWBORN CAPS

A baby's first cap is an item cherished by most parents and makes a special addition to any baby album. Some infants wear the hat for a very short time and others wear it much longer, but it is usually the first item of clothing put on a newborn, making it memorable and noteworthy.

THE HAT
Supplies: Patterned papers (Carolee's Creations); wood accent (EK Success); wood letters (Westrim); letter stickers (American Crafts, Boxer Scrapbook Productions); heart brad (Provo Craft); ribbon (May Arts); cardstock

BABY BRACELETS, PRINTS AND ULTRASOUNDS

I was a whole lot surprised when baby number three came out with dark skin and hair, unlike her older brother and sister. I wanted her to have an account of the conversation that took place right after she was born. The journaling explains the surprised and tired look on my face, and the hospital bracelet, tiny footprint and copy of her ultrasound reinforce that she really does belong in this family.

SWAPPED AT BIRTH
Supplies: Patterned papers (SEI); die-cut letters (QuickKutz); paper flowers (Prima); fabric label (Me & My Big Ideas); chalk (Pebbles); eyelets (Making Memories); cardstock

BABY GIFT CARDS

One way to save tiny baby cards is in specially made strip pockets. The pockets are quick and easy to make and allow several cards to be shown at once, while still making it easy to remove them and read the messages they contain.

WELCOME HOME
Supplies: Patterned papers, letter stickers (SEI); paper flower (Prima)

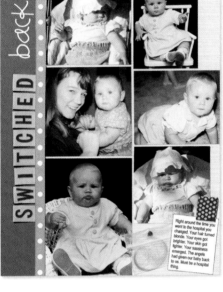

SAVE LITTLE TAGS AND
PINS FOR PERFECT
THEME PAGE ACCENTS

BABIES' HAIR COLOR
CAN CHANGE FAST;
SAVE LOCKETS TO
DOCUMENT CHANGE

BABY MEMORABILIA

Here are some of the many
baby items that can be saved
and included in a baby book:

O Baby food labels

O Baby socks

O Bedding set fabric

O Birth announcement

O Birth certificate

O Blanket scraps

O Cards and letters

O Favorite outfit

O Foot- and handprints

O Hospital bracelet

O Hospital cap

O Lockets of hair

O Name bracelet

O Name origin

O Newborn diaper

O Newspaper clippings

O Shower gift wrap

O Ultrasound image

BIRTH CERTIFICATES

Poor Joani remained unnamed for five long days,
and sharing that story on the page that includes
her birth certificate, which declares her name,
seemed just right. Because the information shown
on her birth certificate doesn't need to be seen by
all who look at her album, I tucked it in its own envelope on the back of the page. Not only is she able
to read about her story, she has a duplicate copy of
her birth certificate should she ever need it.

BABY ?

*Supplies: Letter stickers (Scrapworks); market tag (Pebbles);
safety pins (Making Memories); cardstock*

LOCKETS OF HAIR

When no photos of a specific event are
available, items can be added to layouts that
include photos taken during the same time
frame. My husband didn't think to take pictures
when Joani got her first haircut (from her older
brother) but he did save a piece of the hair. Because the clipped hair is blond, it matches the
storyline shared here. It made sense to include
the hair on this page.

SWITCHED BACK

*Supplies: Patterned paper (KI Memories); fabric labels (Scrap-
works); letter stickers (American Crafts); brad (Bazzill); ribbon
(May Arts); cardstock; stamping ink*

collections album

As a whole, folks in this country love to collect things. I don't know if that stems from a passion for shopping, an urge to be surrounded by items that bring us joy or from the desire to own "stuff."

In 1980 I became obsessed with stuffed bears. Not necessarily the ones found in any toy store and loved by children worldwide, but designer bears...collector bears. For years I'd receive them as birthday and Christmas gifts, adding to my already-full shelves. Now, 25 years later, my stuffed friends live in a huge Rubbermaid tub stored in the attic. An album is a perfect place to save and store the special memories those bears hold.

A simple album, or pages within an album, can save what I want, be easily accessible and honor what really matters. So, when thinking about how to save all those small and large family treasures, while still having room to live, consider using bits and pieces of them in your scrapbooks.

FLAT ITEMS MAKE GREAT EMBELLISHMENTS THAT CAN BE PUNCHED OR STITCHED DIRECTLY ONTO THE SCRAPBOOK PAGE

IN SOME CASES, MEMORABILIA CAN BE TIED OR ATTACHED TO THE PAGE WITH THE MEMORABILIA ITSELF, SUCH IS THE CASE WITH MANY CRAFT ITEMS

IF YOU'RE NOT ABLE TO SCRAP A 3-D COLLECTIBLE, SAVE THE CATALOG YOU ORDER THEM FROM TO EMBELLISH YOUR PAGES

COLLECTIBLE CARDS

Showcase trading cards by tucking them into a clear, PVC-free plastic pocket mounted on the page with tiny eyelets.

49ER CARDS
Supplies: Rub-on letters (Making Memories); pocket (Karen Foster Design)

RIBBON

Feature little snippets of your textile collection by punching holes directly in the page and tying ribbon into knots.

RIBBON
Supplies: Rub-on letters (Making Memories); ribbon (May Arts, Offray)

MANUFACTURER HISTORY

Vellum pockets are a handy little place to tuck literature and booklets from the product manufacturers of your favorite collectibles.

BASKETS
Supplies: Rub-on letters (Making Memories); vellum pocket

Pages of this sort often benefit from a simple approach. Journaling, photos and the saved pieces of memorabilia are often more than enough to safely and effectively capture the memories, tell the stories and allow present and future generations to enjoy the collections.

When Jones was about 18 months old the Disney movie "Pocahontas" came out. With three kids under age five we watched a whole lot of Disney and all new releases were eagerly awaited. As soon as we saw the movie we knew they'd based the character "Meeko" after our baby girl. The two had a whole lot in common. A new nick name, and the beginning of a collection that has lasted 11 years to date, was born.

TAGS ARE THE BEST WAY TO REMEMBER WHERE YOUR FAVORITE COLLECTIBLE CAME FROM AND OFTEN CONTAIN LIMITED-EDITION OR TITLE IN-FORMATION ON COLLECTIBLES

MANUFACTURER TAGS

Brads provide a simple way to mount product manufacturer tags from your collection directly on a page.

BASKETS
Supplies: Rub-on letters (Making Memories); brads (Bazzill)

COLLECTIBLE MEMORABILIA

Almost any type of collectible item can be saved in an album. Certainly, large pieces of furniture won't fit, but photos of them will, as will bits of the fabric and the invoices or tags that accompany them. Be creative; if it matters to you and a piece of it can be saved, save it. Here are just a few of the many collectible items that can be housed in a scrapbook:

- Art; copies or small versions of the real thing
- Baskets
- Bottle caps
- Buttons, sewing notions
- Cameras, lenses, filters
- Depression glass, dishes
- Figurines
- Flowers, leaves, feathers
- Frames
- Garden-seed packets, stakes
- Gems, rocks, wood
- Guns, knives
- Hats
- Jewelry, brooches
- LPs, CDs
- Matchbooks
- Pens
- Pins, patches
- Postcards
- Spoons, silverware
- Stamps, old letters
- Stuffed toys
- Trading, sports cards

hobby album

One aspect of all our lives that tends to get overlooked in our albums are the hobbies we participate in, what we do in our spare or down time. Many scrapbookers are a little more careful about including our scrapbooking escapades in our personal books, but what about all the other things that we or the various members of our family enjoy? As I firmly believe that a person's choice of hobbies tells a lot about that person, including hobby information in our albums can help give both current and future generations a clearer picture of an individual's personality.

HAVE MATERIALS LEFT OVER FROM A SPECIAL PROJECT? USE THE REMNANTS TO EMBELLISH A SCRAPBOOK PAGE

TUCK YOUR HOBBY SOURCES NEATLY BEHIND PHOTOS TO KEEP CLOSE AT HAND

KEEP TINY MEMENTOS OF FAVORITE PRODUCTS, PEOPLE AND PLACES FOR HOBBY-PAGE ACCENTS

FABRIC SCRAPS

My mom is a quilter, and that takes up a huge portion of her free time. There are many different aspects involved with most hobbies, and this one is no different. In my mom's case, the events she participates in, trips she has taken or places she has visited because of her hobby are featured. Leftover fabric scraps or swatches are the perfect, custom-coordinated page accent when showcasing hobby photos of the actual project.

WINTER DAZZLE
Supplies used for all pages: Patterned paper (Patchwork Paper Design); die-cut letters, shapes (QuicKutz); eyelets, brads, snowflake, tag (Making Memories); leaf (Karen Foster Design); glassine envelope (Little Black Dress Designs); ribbon (May Arts); cardstock

HIDDEN BUSINESS CARDS

Create a hidden-pocket page behind photos. Then mount business cards and personal hobby contacts related to specific projects on cardstock, add a ribboned pull tab, and slide discreetly in pocket behind photos for safekeeping. In my mom's case, she also uses her book as a resource guide. With each quilt made, she learns something new. She jots that down and keeps a record of it, for herself in case she makes the same quilt again, and so she can pass the information along to her many quilting friends.

RESOURCES
Supplies: See list at left.

PERSONAL PREFERENCES

In every hobby or craft, there are products, people and places that we prefer over others. Keep little reminders of these preferences for highly personal page remembrances. Her favorite companies, manufacturers, stores and people, along with the awards she has won, projects she has been hired to do, classes she has taught and friends she has made because of her hobby are important. Those are just a few of the things that could be included in her album about quilting.

FAVORITES
Supplies: See list at left.

One of the beauties of including hobby information in our books is that it can be done in many different ways. An entire album, large or small, can be devoted to all the hobbies enjoyed by different family members. A page or more can be made for each hobby to be included in general family albums. Specialty albums, in any size, can be made for any specific hobby. My point is that the options are endless and the benefit is huge. Decide on a format and have fun!

HOBBY MEMORABILIA

Here are just a few of the many things that can be included in your album or on your pages about hobbies:

- O Awards
- O Building or creation tips
- O Convention or trade show slips
- O Directions, patterns or plans
- O Fliers or brochures about products or events
- O Pieces of items used in the hobby
- O Publications received or subscribed to
- O Tags or receipts from items purchased
- O Tools needed

This pattern, by "Little Stitches" was found at the NW Quilters show in Vancouver, WA. A Longview vendor, "Momma Made It" sold the kit and a few of mom's friends bought it. The kit included the pattern and enough fabric for the top. My clever mom pieced together the scraps to make the back and she started just before going to HIA in Dallas with me. She finished the top on Feb. 12, 2004, just after returning from the show.

ATTACH YOUR MEMORA-BILIA IN A WAY THAT'S APPROPRIATE FOR YOUR HOBBY. SHOWN HERE ARE QUILTING MATERIALS STITCHED ON THE PAGE

SHOW CRAFT IN USE

Use your hobby to mount and adhere souvenirs and mementos to the page. In this case, stitching is used for a quilting page. Any type of needle-work also works well on craft pages. The entire book (ok, several books!) could include just the quilts my mom has made, along with pieces of the fabrics she used, who she gave the quilts to, the patterns used to make the quilts and the dates she started and finished them.

CHICKEN LITTLE
Supplies: See list at left.

holiday album

Holidays. We celebrate the same ones each year, and we relish in the traditions they bring, both new and old. Each of the holidays offers its own sort of memorabilia—from egg holders used during Easter to flags proudly waved on July 4th. Those tangible bits found with each holiday make wonderful page accents, and they help cement the feel of tradition on the pages they grace. Whether you create an entire album dedicated to one specific holiday or you use saved treasures on the pages that go in your family albums, be sure to save some of those items that help make your holidays complete.

OTHER IDEAS FOR YOUR ALBUM TITLE PAGE CAN INCLUDE A CHRISTMAS WISH FROM EACH MEMBER OF THE FAMILY OR THEN AND NOW IMAGES

CONSIDER EMBELLISHING PHOTO CARDS WITH FRAMES OR CREATING A MINIATURE PHOTO ALBUM YOU CAN MOUNT ON YOUR SCRAPBOOK PAGE

BEGIN AND END YOUR ALBUMS BASED ON TRADITIONAL BOOK THEMES SUCH AS "ONCE UPON A TIME" & "THEY LIVED HAPPILY EVER AFTER"

ALBUM TITLE PAGE

My favorite part of each Christmas season comes in the mailbox. The holiday cards and letters allow me an annual glimpse into the lives of those I love yet am unable to spend much time with. By putting those special greetings in an album of their own, I'm able to enjoy the cards and letters all over again. Each year a different Christmas song is used for the title and the words to that song are included on the layout. The first page of the book tells why I love Christmas letters...

CHRISTMAS FAVORITES

Supplies: Patterned papers (Flair Designs, Paper Adventures, Paper Fever); tags, buttons (Making Memories); ribbon (May Arts); brads (ScrapArts); letter stickers (Doodlebug Design); word stickers (O'Scrap); die-cut letters (QuicKutz)

PHOTO CARDS

On this page the cards and photos are attached directly to the background paper, acting as their own mats and embellishments. Considering the volume of cards and letters that can be included in a project like this, it is important to keep the lines simple and the embellishments to a minimum.

JOY TO THE WORLD

Supplies: Die-cut letters (QuicKutz); metal tree (Making Memories); ribbon (May Arts); cardstock

ALBUM END PAGE

...and the last page is the story 'Twas the Night Before Christmas.

AND TO ALL A GOOD NIGHT

Supplies: Patterned papers (Flair Designs, Keeping Memories Alive); paper-pieced Santa template (source unknown); cardstock

HOLIDAY MEMORABILIA

Here are just a few of the many holiday treasures that can be saved in albums:

○ Bottle tops

○ Bows and ribbon

○ Cards and letters

○ Confetti

○ Costume parts and pieces

○ Flags

○ Flower petals or leaves

○ Gift tags and labels

○ Miniature decorations

○ Party hats, favors and blowers

○ Party invitations

○ Product boxes and packages

○ Wine or holiday food labels

○ Wrapping paper

RECYCLE A HOLIDAY ENVELOPE BY USING IT ON A SCRAPBOOK PAGE TO HOLD PICTURES, TOY INSTRUCTIONS, JOURNALING, TAGS AND OTHER HOLIDAY MEMORABILIA

CHRISTMAS-CARD POCKET

Using a Christmas card as a pocket is a great way to save space and feature a handmade card. Because the card was only sewn to the page on the inside lip of the card, it can still be opened and its message can be reread.

HOLLY JOLLY CHRISTMAS

Supplies: Sticker (O'Scrap); ribbon (May Arts); brad (ScrapArts); letter embellishments (Colorbök, Creative Imaginations, Li'l Davis Designs, Making Memories, Scrapworks, Scrapyard 329); cardstock

school album

The events and activities associated with education play an integral role in all our lives. The amount of school stuff we save probably runs a close second to the amount of vacation paraphernalia we keep. Sorting through the piles and creatively saving the papers, awards, notes and art can be a challenge. I encourage you to keep in mind the concepts found in the seven main chapters. Using a variety of those basic principles will help you save important and memorable school items as well keep each year's pages from looking the same. So, save that test with a perfect score. Keep your progress reports and report cards. Tuck away awards, student body cards and pictures of teachers and friends. All can be safely and conveniently stored within the pages in your albums.

CREATE A SCHOOL TIMELINE BY SHOWING A PROGRESSION THROUGH HOMEWORK; CONTRASTING PENMANSHIP CAN SHOW MATURITY AS WELL AS ACHIEVEMENT

DON'T BE AFRAID TO CLIP OR MANIPULATE AN AWARD IF YOU WANT TO DISPLAY IT ON A SCRAPBOOK PAGE

WHAT DOES THE REPORT CARD TELL YOU? CREATE A PAGE BASED ON AN AREA YOUR CHILD EXCEEDS IN

HOMEWORK ASSIGNMENTS

Some assignments make a bigger impact than others and require creative effort outside of class to complete. Saving pieces from those types of assignments not only make wonderful accents, they bring the memory and story to life.

HISTORY, LIVE
Supplies: Twill letters, buttonhole tape (Carolee's Creations); letter stickers (Doodlebug Design); brads (Bazzill); cardstock

AWARD DOCUMENTS

Paper awards can cause one of the greatest challenges when saving school-related items. Usually they don't match other awards from the same period. They have lots of "empty" space on them. Left in frames on walls, they collect dust. They are often large so take up a good chunk of room on a page. Most of them can conveniently be tucked in pouches, envelopes and pockets and then taken out to enjoy and tucked back in for safekeeping. Occasionally an award merits its own page. In this case I wanted the award to be prominent yet still have room for other items.

AMY DAHMEN
Supplies: Patterned papers (Basic Grey); die-cut heart (Quic-Kutz); photo turn (Making Memories); plastic pocket (Karen Foster Design); brad (ScrapArts); ribbon (Beaux Regards); stamping ink; cardstock

REPORT CARDS

Sometimes certain items deserve a special place of their own. Report cards are thin and fit nicely in this accordion-style envelope. Readily available, yet not in direct sight, they don't compete with the fabulous photo taken of her during the school year.

SMART LOVE BUG
Supplies: Patterned papers (KI Memories); letter stickers (American Crafts, Doodlebug Design, KI Memories); ribbon (Beaux Regards); button (Making Memories)

SCHOOL MEMORABILIA

Keep the memorabilia that's important to your child and your child's school experience for meaningful page additions. Consider photographing or scanning an overabundance of memorabilia for your album if necessary. Some items to keep include:

O Artwork

O Certificates, ribbons and awards

O Class schedules

O Copies of textbook covers

O Graded homework

O Handprints

O Handwriting samples

O Meaningful doodles and drawings

O News clippings

O Notes from teachers and classmates

O Programs and special-event fliers

O Receipts

O Report cards

O School supplies

O Special test scores

O Ticket stubs

KEEP AWARDS ORGANIZED BY CREATING FOLDERS OR MINI ALBUMS WITH DIFFERENT THEMES, SUCH AS SCHOOL ACTIVITES OR GRADE LEVELS

SCHOOLWORK

Back to the four kids thing: I want to save items from each school year for each child. I think it is important for them to be able to look back, see where they were, see how they've changed and note the progress they've made. But, I don't want them to need a U-Haul to tote their albums when they move away from home. So each child gets from two to six layouts per school year, depending on what they did, how pivotal that year was and how much needs to be saved to tell their stories. Here I combined the first-day-of-school picture with samples of work done throughout the year. It takes very little space, is a varied offering of what topics were covered and allows Amy to go back at her convenience to remember the eighth grade.

SCHOOLWORK

Supplies: Patterned papers (Sweetwater); die-cut letters (QuickKutz); ribbon (Beaux Regards, May Arts, Making Memories)

showcase variations

Many frequently saved items make wonderful page accents as they enhance the mood of the page. A number of scrapbookers find that they save the same thing over and over again, such as sand from the various beach vacations. Finding unique ways to showcase the same item can be a challenge, but here are some ideas to get you started. Showcasing some of those items—such as sand, for example—on a layout can be tricky as it is fine and easily escapes most containers, which can scratch your photos. To display successfully, use small amounts.

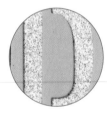

ATTACH A PLASTIC BAG BY TYING RIBBONS, WIRE OR FISHING LINE AROUND A DECORATIVE BRAD

ACTUALLY MOUNT THE GRITTY SOUVENIR ON PAPER TO USE AS A PAGE ACCENT

TRANSLUCENT ENVELOPES DISPLAY AND PRESERVE YOUR MEMORABILIA WITHOUT HAVING TO REMOVE IT FOR VIEWING

MINI ZIPPERED BAGS

Sand in a plastic bag makes just the right embellishment for a day spent watching pros build sand castles. It is a simple and effective embellishment, and the color and type of sand found at the beach is saved for all to remember.

SAND CASTLES

Supplies: Vellum, plastic letters (Déjà Views); letter stickers (Doodlebug Design); label (Me & My Big Ideas); brads (ScrapArts); twill, ribbon (May Arts); die-cut tag topper (QuicKutz); tag (Making Memories); cardstock

TITLE ACCENT

Sand adds texture and dimension to any layout and helps bring this title to life. To make the title, I first sanded and painted the negative space found in chipboard letters. When the paint was dry, I cut solid white cardstock to fit the back of each letter. Doing one letter at a time, I sprayed the cardstock with adhesive and placed it on the back of the chipboard letter. Before it dried I sprinkled a small amount of sand in the empty space, shaking it around until the sand covered all the white space inside the letter. I tapped the excess sand out of the letter and allowed it to dry completely. I followed the same process for each letter and glued them in place on the page when the adhesive was completely dry.

WONDERFUL SAND

Supplies: Patterned papers, stickers, ribbon (SEI); chipboard stencils (Rusty Pickle); acrylic paint

PREMADE ENVELOPES AND ENCLOSURES

Premade envelopes and enclosures work well to hold small items like this. The key here was to use enough Super Tape to keep the entire lip closed underneath the envelope flap. Even a small gap will allow minute particles of sand to escape. The tape is strong enough to keep the sand in place; it just has to be cut to the correct dimension.

SANDBOX BABY

Supplies: Patterned paper (Scrapworks); envelope (EK Success); stickers (Chatterbox); cardstock

From the first time you played in a sandbox we knew you were a sand crab. You immediately bent down, using your hands as shovels, to dig in the soft sand. Over the years you did your best to live up to that early reputation. Every time we'd go to the beach, a park or any place with sand you'd bend and dig. Just like a little sand crab. '96

MINIATURE MEMORABILIA

Many small and finely ground items work well on layouts and can enhance the theme of the page; here are just a few of them:

O Confetti

O Grain

O Rice

O Sand

O Seeds of all kinds

O Spices

Refer to Chapter 6, Shakers & Frames, pages 56-61 for additional ideas for packaging mini memorabilia.

USE THIS CONCEPT WITH OTHER ALBUM IDEAS TO HOLD CONFETTI, DRIED FLOWERS AND OTHER FOUND ITEMS

MINI TAG SHAKER BOX

The plain market tags made a great background for the title letters, and I wanted to carry that out with a home for the sand and the little die-cut crab. I used a large circle punch to make the hole and I placed a clear, tiny zipper bag behind the hole to house the sand and crab. I used Super Tape to hold the bag in place and the tight zipper seal ensures the sand will stay inside the bag.

SAND CRAB
Supplies: Patterned papers, stickers (Chatterbox); brads, zipper plastic bag (ScrapArts); market tags (Pebbles); ribbon (May Arts); die cut (Li'l Davis Designs)

theme variations

Sometimes an idea or layout concept strikes you just right. It works for you. It sings to you. It inspires you to try new and different things. When that happens, take the idea, twist it and turn it and get the most mileage possible from it. These layouts were all created based on that idea. I saw a greeting card at the store that was perfect in its simplicity. A slimly matted rectangular picture of a sleeping newborn was placed over four different strips of color. In the lower corner was the word "congratulations." I knew the concept would work well for layouts by changing the memorabilia items beneath the photo. The pages shown here are just the beginning—one small look at the many varied things you can create from the same simple design idea.

GARAGE SALES AND FLEA MARKETS ARE GREAT PLACES TO FIND OLD, FAMILIAR BOOKS

SAVE GIFT TAGS AND SWATCHES OF YOUR FAVORITE WRAPPING PAPER TO PERSONALIZE YOUR HOLIDAY PAGES

SELECTING YOUR COLOR PALETTE IS EASY WHEN YOU TAKE THE LEAD FROM PREMADE GIFT CARDS

OLD BOOK PAGES

Love books? Us too. In fact, they make up a huge part of our daily lives. When a book is worn out, torn or missing pertinent information, I have a hard time throwing it away. By using pages and sections from old, seemingly useless books I can save a small part of something that is very important to my family.

READ
Supplies: Book pages (Children's Bible, Curious George); tag (Making Memories); ribbon (May Arts); brad (ScrapArts); letter stamps (Hero Arts); cardstock

GIFT WRAP

I buy different wrapping paper for each family member. By wrapping each person's gifts, especially the small items that fill our stockings, in the same paper, it is less likely that an item will get placed in the wrong pile. I used scraps from the kids' papers for a background on this page of them with their aunt and grandparents in matching Christmas pajamas. The picture will make them smile and the scraps will help them remember which pattern was their own.

MAGIC CHRISTMAS
Supplies: Gift wrap (Target); title (Memories Complete); date stamp (Office Depot); ribbon (May Arts); cardstock; stamping ink

GIFT CARDS

One item many of us routinely save are the greeting cards we receive for birthdays, holidays and other special occasions. Coming up with unique and special ways to showcase those cards can present quite a challenge. For this page, which includes one of the few photos of my oldest daughter as a newborn, I used the front of a few baby greetings to make the background. The messages found inside the cards were cut off and saved in a pocket on a subsequent page.

GOD'S HEART
Supplies: Baby gift and greeting cards; cardstock

THEME VARIATION TOPICS

When you find a page-design that you like, think about how you might be able to use it again on another page with a different theme. Some theme topics to consider:

O Baby
O Birthday
O Child
O Family
O Friends
O Heritage
O Holiday
O Portrait
O School Days
O Seasons
O Sports
O Traditions
O Travel
O Wedding

FEEL SAD TAKING PRIZED HOMEWORK OFF THE FRIDGE? CREATE A FOLDER TO HOLD SCHOOL PROJECTS TO USE LATER AS BACKGROUNDS OR PAGE EMBELLISHMENTS

SCHOOLWORK

One sheet of schoolwork from each of the children made the background for this page, showing a glimpse of their personalities, handwriting and what they did in school at that age. The kids will have a piece of their own work, as well as a look at where their siblings were at that same time. Another twist on the same idea is to use a section of schoolwork from one child for each of the subjects taken that year. It can act as an introduction to the school pages saved for that grade or it can show an overview of the type of work done during that era and time frame.

SCHOOLWORK '04

Supplies: Letter stickers (Debbie Mumm, Doodlebug Design); cardstock

vacation album

Vacations are events that can generate an incredible amount of memorabilia. From postcards to coins, ticket stubs to brochures, all can help save the memories and share the stories. The challenge then is to come up with different and interesting ways to scrapbook the same event, either for different albums or for multiple pages in a single album, in unique ways.

SOMETIMES THE BEST SOUVENIRS ARE THE FOUND OBJECTS DISCOVERED DURING THE JOURNEY. SHOWCASE THEM IN SMALL, CLEAR POCKETS

THE FUN THAT MEMORA- BILIA ADDS TO SCRAPBOOKS IS GETTING TO OPEN UP THE ENVELOPES HOLDING YOUR SECRET TREASURES

PRESERVE LOOSE MEMORABILIA IN STYLISH CONTAINERS THAT CAN BE TIED ON WITH RIBBON

FLORA AND FAUNA

Pressed flowers and leaves from vacation spots make great and inexpensive (free!) page addi- tions. Press them in a book until you get home, and let them dry completely before using. Pressed flowers and leaves are fragile; to "mend" something like this tiny maple leaf, simply use tweezers and a tiny dab of archival glue to "fix" it. There are other ways to stretch your buck. Scrapbook supplies can be costly, and re-purpos- ing them to make them go farther can be a great way to save money. For two of the pages here I used one package of die-cut words and split it. The words "O Canada" came in a laser-die pack from Li'l Davis Designs, and it contained two sheets. The first was an empty centered overlay...

TRIP TO CANADA
Supplies: Rub-on letters, metal date (Making Memories); die-cut word and shapes (Li'l Davis Designs); brads (ScrapArts); plastic pocket (Karen Foster Design); cardstock

SOUVENIR PINS

...and the second, meant to be the back piece, was white and slightly wider. It was designed to create a layered effect. I used just the overlay as a portion of the title on the "Canada Trip" layout and then the background piece was inked black and used on the "Trip to Canada" layout. With the need to create many layouts, little money-saving tips such as this can go a long way in stretching your scrapbook dollar. Note how the souvenir pin and handmade flag pull the country's colors of red and white from the photos.

CANADA TRIP
Supplies: Die-cut word and flag (Li'l Davis Designs); tags (QuicKutz); brads (ScrapArts); eyelets (Making Memories); glassine envelope (Little Black Dress Designs); rub-on letters (Doodlebug Design, KI Memories); cardstock

REPETITIVE KEEPSAKES

Since I have four children, and each child has albums of his or her own, I face the challenge of creating layouts that look different for each of their albums. While the styles are somewhat similar, on each of these layouts the same mem- orabilia is saved in different ways. For the far left page, I used a ready-made plastic pocket. The page at right uses the coins as the only page embellishment. The page on the immediate left shows how a simple glassine envelope can creatively hold small treasures, and this layout uses another ready-made product: a keepsake holder. By varying the ways you save your trea- sures, you can create interest and offer variety.

CANADA '99
Supplies: Memorabilia holder (Pebbles); rub-ons (Making Memories); brads (ScrapArts); ribbon (May Arts); cardstock

Our final destination on the all-family trip. We spent two days in Victoria, BC and it was incredible. All four of you loved the carriage ride around the city. Not because of the history or sights, but because of the horses. You enjoyed watching them. At one point Molly (the feisty one) bit Bart (the pacifist) and that was a major highlight. Even now, 6 years later, you guys will say "Mom, Molly bit Bart!" when we see Clydesdales. You and Jones both want to go back someday so you can "do" tea at the Empress with Grama. Touted as home to "flower beds, newlyweds and nearly deads", Victoria is truly a beautiful city and the boat trips to see Orca pods just make it all the more desirable as a great vacation destination.

Vacation: **CANADA**

'99

MEMORIALIZE YOUR TRAVELS WITH FOREIGN COINS DATED IN THE YEAR OF YOUR VISIT

'99

COIN OPTION

Though not done here, coins can be tied onto a page. Creating a hole in a coin is fairly easy with the right tools. Use a glue dot or small piece of adhesive to tack your coin to a scrap piece of wood. Make sure the wood is securely clamped or is large enough (like a work bench) that your base won't move while being drilled. Select a fine, narrow drill bit (1/16 is a good size); hold the drill at a 90-degree angle and drill through the coin. Be sure to wear safety glasses as small bits of metal can cause damage. Some countries have made it illegal to deface or destroy coins. Check local rules prior to making a hole.

VACATION: CANADA
Supplies: Rub-on letters (Making Memories); ribbon (May Arts); coin adhesive (Therm O Web); cardstock

VACATION MEMORABILIA

Here are a few of the items from a vacation that can be saved and used to enhance an album:

O Coins or money used in that area

O Country flag

O Envelope or postage

O Hotel or room keys

O Jewelry or fabric or any product created in that location

O Local dried flowers or leaves

O Location brochures

O Menus

O Passport

O Pens

O Postcards

O Receipts

O Souvenir bags

O Stationery

O Tickets, stubs, tokens and passes

O Travel logs or pages

wedding album

Wedding photos and wedding memorabilia are the most challenging to scrapbook. Whether it is the emotion behind this once-in-a-lifetime event or the nature of the photos and keepsakes themselves, putting together a wedding album can be daunting. However, including memorabilia on the pages with those special photos will help make the story unfold in your own personal style. And often the most simple formula—understated paper, a few accents and some ribbon or flowers will help simplify the process.

SAVE INVITIATIONS AND BULLETINS YOU RECEIVE FROM DIFFERENT EVENTS TO SAVE TIME ON JOURNALING

TAKE SONG TITLES AND QUOTED SCRIPTURE FROM THE WEDDING PROGRAM TO USE AS TITLES FOR YOUR PAGE

REFER TO CHAPTER 6 TO CREATE SHAKERS AND FRAMES CONTAINING LOOSE PARTY FAVORS FROM YOUR EVENT

INVITATION

A great deal of time is usually spent on invitation selection. The mood of the wedding is often determined by the font, style, paper and word choice found on the invitations. Allowing that slip of paper to help you set the tone for the layout is a great way to get started on making your wedding pages. By tucking the invitation under the main photo—and pairing it with some torn vellum, ink, ribbon, velvet paper and a few flowers—I've let the understated elegance of the invitation determine the direction of the remaining pages. Because the invitation can't be opened, a second invitation was included in a pocket on the back so the greeting could be read.

CEREMONY

For some this might be a place for the marriage license or wedding certificate, but our pastor gave us a booklet with our names and the words used to form our wedding service. The large expanse of white found on the book cover presented a challenge, as I wanted to ensure the book could be opened and read. A simple velvet pocket allows both easy access and a nice color contrast. I found that allowing the memorabilia to take equal importance on the pages helped me break up the pages into categories and subtopics.

FAVORS

My bridesmaids spent hours helping me make our fun wedding favors. I bought See's caramel lollipops, wrapped them in white tulle, tied them with dark blue ribbon and added a tag with our names and date. Very simple and very tasty. We had a great time together making those, and many guests enjoyed the unique treat. Saving the lollipop in the album wasn't feasible, but using the ribbon and tag as a page accent works wonderfully, even though the actual lollipops can't be seen in the photo used.

WEDDING MEMORABILIA

Wedding pages offer many opportunities to include bits and pieces of the memorabilia that surrounds such an event. Here are just a few of the items that can be included and help make your wedding album complete:

○ Ads that inspired choices

○ Engagement announcement

○ Favors

○ Garter

○ Honeymoon tickets and brochures

○ Invitation

○ Newspaper clipping

○ Petals

○ Planner pages

○ Pressed flowers

○ Program

○ Receipts

○ Ribbons from showers and gifts

○ Rice or birdseed

○ RSVP cards

○ Table and seating cards

○ Wine, champagne and food labels

○ Wrapping paper

USING THE SAME CONCEPT, SCRAPBOOK CARDS YOU RECEIVE FROM YOUR ENGAGEMENT PARTY AND BRIDAL SHOWER

GUESTS

The whole wedding experience was made more special, enjoyable and memorable because of the people who attended and offered us their blessings. A large vellum envelope allowed me to include the two-sided page from our guest book with the photos of our guests. (And, if you look REALLY close, in the center top photo you can see a See's lollipop in the hand of one of the two little redheaded boys.)

Contributing artists

These ladies are some of the most talented, creative and gifted scrapbookers I've ever been lucky enough to know. Even more important, they are genuine, sincere and incredibly good people. Each has a distinct and notable style, and while their individual looks are very different, every one of them continually teaches and challenges me to think outside of the box while creating my own layouts. I'm constantly learning from them, and their willingness to share their talent has allowed me to grow as both a scrapbooker and a person. I've no doubt you will be as motivated and inspired by their work as I am.

ANGELIA WIGGINTON

With elegance and flair, Angelia conveys her love for her children and family in her layouts. She is incredibly gifted at combining patterned papers and utilizing ready-made product. She adds a touch of her warm personality to all she creates. Angelia lives in Belmont, Mississippi, with her two beautiful girls and her husband, Rich. Scrapbooking since 1998, she was recently named a 2006 Memory Makers Master. She is a former member of the 2004 Paper Kuts Power Team and has been widely published. She now creates stunning layouts for Me & My BIG ideas and is on the K & Company design team. More of her layouts can be seen at www.downmemorylaneco.com.

DENISE TUCKER

A longtime resident of Versailles, Indiana, Denise is a special education teacher and mother of four. She and her husband, Trace, have been married for over 20 years, and she has been scrapbooking since 1997. Denise is the texture queen, and the amount of love she incorporates into every page always inspires me to try to include more depth and meaning in my own work. She has an amazing knack for picking up on the strengths and weaknesses in layouts, and she can always be counted on to offer constructive, honest and helpful advice. She was inducted as a Memory Makers Master in 2004, and she now does fabulous design teamwork for CR Gibson and Rusty Pickle.

DIANA HUDSON

The most charming and infectious laugh I've ever heard comes from the tiny form of Diana. She creates paper and product for Carolee's Creations, and her "love worn" line offers a glimpse of her bubbly and vivacious personality. She is an Oklahoma native but now resides in Bakersfield, California, with her son, daughter and husband, Curtis. She began scrapbooking eons ago and was selected as a Memory Makers Master in 2003. Each of her layouts shines with the warmth she exudes, and Diana is fantastic about trying every new product and technique that hits the industry.

ELIZABETH RUUSKA

I am convinced that Elizabeth is a saint. She home schools her nine children in rural Rensselear, Indiana, where she lives with her kids and husband, Eric. The love and respect she has for her family are integral parts of all the pages she creates, and her children's personalities show in the design and flow of her work. She draws inspiration from the most amazing things, and I'm fairly sure she was the impetus behind the term "think outside the box." Scrapbooking allows Elizabeth to blend the things she loves most: writing, photography, design and her family. A previous Creating Keepsakes Hall of Fame winner, she now works with the Junkitz design team and shows others how fun and versatile that product line is.

KELLI NOTO

Photographer and "friend extraordinaire" concisely sums up Kelli. A simple and streamlined scrapbooker, she willingly admits that she wants her sublime photos to take center stage on her pages. A 12 x 15" scrapbooker, she adds little bits and twists that make her photos pop out and her layouts shine. A former schoolteacher, Kelli lives in Centennial, Colorado, with her husband, John, and their two boys. She was a Memory Makers Master in 2003, and she now writes a photography tip column for that magazine. Kelli bakes delicious M&M cookies, does a variety of volunteer work, and she graces the QuicKutz team with her innovative use of their die cuts.

PAM KOPKA

What can I say about Pam? Her art just blows me away. She takes common art elements and incorporates them in her scrapbook pages in ways that are truly unique, amazing and inspiring. If she is intrigued by something, if she likes the look, she does it. No rules, no games. A kindergarten teacher, she resides in tiny New Galilee, Pennsylvania, with her husband, Denny, and her two darling daughters. Pam's love of art started at a young age, and she has been scrapbooking for 12 years. She was selected for the 2004 Creating Keepsakes Hall of Fame, and her work has been published industrywide.

SHELLEY LAMING

Our "newlywed" Shelley is known for her amazing skill at combining bold color with style and innovation. She currently spends most of her time at home in Fountain Inn, South Carolina, where she, her husband Ned, and their two darling girls are remodeling their house. Shelley is a former Creating Keepsakes Hall of Fame winner and a Garden Girl on www.TwoPeasinaBucket.com. She showed the Internet scrapbooking world that effective layouts can be simple as well as compelling and beautiful. Her "random words of advice" layouts have taught me to more carefully consider what message I want to share with my family and to accept that depth and meaning can be both lighthearted and fun.

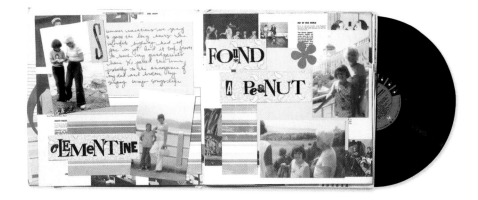

PAGE 12

Additional instructions & credits

PAGE 1 THE BOXCAR CHILDREN
Supplies: Patterned paper (Basic Grey); art supply box (Darice); label holder (Making Memories); decoupage medium (Plaid); cardstock; acrylic paint

PAGE 3 SHELL SHAKER BOOKPLATE
Denise Tucker
Supplies: Patterned papers (Daisy D's, K & Company); metal paper (EK Success); metal molding, ribbon (Making Memories); glass bottle (7 Gypsies); transparency (Kodak); shells (Magic Scraps); acrylic paint; postcards; sand; foam core

PAGE 6 TESTIFY TO LOVE
Supplies: Football die cut (Deluxe Designs); heart die cut (Accu-Cut); metal tag (All My Memories); brad (ScrapArts); cardstock; Longaberger card; Dove chocolate wrapper; Starbucks card; lace heart; embossed worry stone; Bible cover; page

PAGE 7
Photo: Flash Digital Portraits, Vancouver, Washington

PAGE 10 J.D.
Supplies: Patterned paper (Basic Grey); white envelopes (DMD); clear envelopes (Dolphin Song); clips, pins (Office Depot); decoupage medium (Plaid); frames (Target)

PAGE 12 BROADWAY'S BEST DUETS
Elizabeth Ruuska
Supplies: Chipboard letters (Li'l Davis Designs); pen; paper, miscellaneous embellishments (Junkitz)

PAGE 20 BABY ALBUM
Angelia Wigginton
Supplies: Album (SEI); patterned papers (Foofala, Mustard Moon); fabric flowers (Foofala); ribbon (May Arts); fabric labels, rub-on words (K & Company); "M" rub-on (Creative Imaginations); pearl buttons

PAGE 28 TANNER
Denise Tucker
Supplies: Patterned papers (Daisy D's, Rusty Pickle); corners (EK Success); rub-ons (Creative Imaginations); decoupage medium (Plaid); stamps (All Night Media); stamping ink

PAGE 36 PAPA GARY
The chipboard letters were made by first removing the centers from the backgrounds. The separated pieces were painted different colors, allowed to dry, sanded and pieced back together. The last name was printed in reverse on a transparency and adhered with spray adhesive over the top of the chipboard letters, then sewn in place.

PAGE 38 FASHION NOT
Angela Wigginton
Supplies: Patterned papers, monogram letters (Basic Grey); vellum (Paper Company); epoxy stitches, metal bar (K & Company); rub-on letters (My Mind's Eye); rub-on weekdays (Autumn Leaves); mini brads (Doodlebug Design); rickrack (Wrights)

PAGE 46 CHERISH ALL THAT IS DEAR
Supplies: Patterned paper (K & Company); twill letters, ribbon (Carolee's Creations); envelopes (DMD); stamping ink (Close To My Heart); stamps (Hero Arts, PSX Design); book card (Boxer Scrapbook Productions); glassine envelope (Little Black Dress Designs); brad (ScrapArts)

PAGE 54 KYLA
To change the silver metal letters to black, I first coated them heavily with Staz-On ink. They were sprinkled with detail clear embossing powder and heat set. They were inked again and covered with more embossing powder and heat set again. Doing the same step twice gave a dark, fully covered, even result.

PAGE 56 SHADOW BOX
Pam Kopka
Supplies: Frame (Rusty Pickle); lace (Making Memories); word stickers (Karen Foster Design); other stickers (K & Company)

PAGE 59 THE FLAMES SHALL NOT HURT THEE
Elizabeth used diamond glaze to create the mounted homes for the broken stained glass. She covered her work surface with waxed paper and held the silver frames in place with repositionable adhesive. She then laid the sections of stained glass inside the frames and filled the remaining space in the center with diamond glaze. Once completely dry, she removed the frames from the waxed paper, lightly sanded any rough edges and adhered them to her page.

PAGE 62 LOVE X 4
The quilted heart clock was pretty easy to make. I used a cardstock die-cut heart as the background and cut a section of an old quilt to fit over it. I used spray adhesive to hold the quilt in place over the cardstock heart, and I trimmed the fabric about ¼", larger than the heart. I sewed the whole thing together then retrimmed the fabric and batting. The clock handles are held in place with a large brad.

Supplies: Frame (EK Success); printed transparency (K & Company); clock arms, wood number (Darice); letter stamps (Making Memories, PSX Design); brads (ScrapArts); cardstock; old watch faces

PAGE 70 EAST COAST VACATION
Supplies: Album and pages, including all brads, eyelets, ribbon, background paper (Colorbök); die-cut letters (QuickKutz); envelopes (DMD); card stock

PAGES 88-89 WEDDING MEMORIES
Supplies: Velvet paper (K & Company); ribbon (Close To My Heart); brads (Lasting Impressions); paper flowers (Prima); vellum; stamping ink

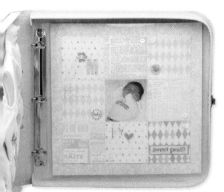

PAGE 20

PAGE 31

PAGE 69

Source guide

The following companies manufacture products featured in this book. Please check your local retailers to find these materials, or go to a company's Web site for the latest product. In addition, we have made every attempt to properly credit the items mentioned in this book. We apologize to any company that we have listed incorrectly, and we would appreciate hearing from you.

3M
(800) 364-3577
www.3m.com

7 Gypsies
(877) 749-7797
www.sevengypsies.com

ACCO Brands
(800) 989-4923
www.acco.com

Accu-Cut®
(800) 288-1670
www.accucut.com

All My Memories
(888) 553-1998
www.allmymemories.com

All Night Media
(see Plaid Enterprises)

American Crafts
(801) 226-0747
www.americancrafts.com

American Tag Company
(800) 223-3956
www.americantag.net

Anna Griffin, Inc.
(888) 817-8170
www.annagriffin.com

Autumn Leaves
(800) 588-6707
www.autumnleaves.com

Basic Grey™
(801) 451-6006
www.basicgrey.com

Bazzill Basics Paper
(480) 558-8557
www.bazzillbasics.com

Beaux Regards
(877) 419-8488
www.beauxregards.com

Berwick Offray, LLC
(800) 344-5533
www.offray.com

Bo-Bunny Press
(801) 771-4010
www.bobunny.com

Boutique Trims, Inc.
(248) 437-2017
www.boutiquetrims.com

Boxer Scrapbook Productions
(503) 625-0455
www.boxerscrapbooks.com

Bunch Of Fun
(877) 419-8488
www.bunchoffun.com

Canson®, Inc.
(800) 628-9283
www.canson-us.com

Carolee's Creations®
(435) 563-1100
www.ccpaper.com

Century
www.centuryplastics.com

Chatterbox, Inc.
(208) 939-9133
www.chatterboxinc.com

Clearsnap, Inc.
(360) 293-6634
www.clearsnap.com

Close To My Heart®
(888) 655-6552
www.closetomyheart.com

Colorbök™, Inc.
(800) 366-4660
www.colorbok.com

Creative Imaginations
(800) 942-6487
www.cigift.com

Creative Impressions Rubber Stamps, Inc.
(719) 596-4860
www.creativeimpressions.com

Creative Memories®
(800) 468-9335
www.creativememories.com

Creek Bank Creations, Inc.
(217) 427-5980
www.creekbankcreations.com

Cut-It-Up™
(530) 389-2233
www.cut-it-up.com

Daisy D's Paper Company
(888) 601-8955
www.daisydspaper.com

Darice, Inc.
(800_ 321-1494
www.darice.com

Debbie Mumm®
(888) 819-2923
www.debbiemumm.com

Dèjá Views
(800) 243-8419
www.dejaviews.com

Deluxe Designs
(480) 497-9005
www.deluxedesigns.com

DMD Industries, Inc.
(800) 805-9890
www.dmdind.com

Dolphin Song - no contact info

Doodlebug Design™ Inc.
(801) 966-9952
www.doodlebug.ws

Duck Products/Henkel Consumer Adhesives, Inc.
(800) 321-0253
www.ducktapeproducts.com

Dymo
(800) 426-7827
www.dymo.com

Eastman Kodak Company
(770) 522-2542
www.kodak.com

EK Success™, Ltd.
(800) 524-1349
www.eksuccess.com

Fibers by the Yard™
(405) 364-8066
www.fibersbytheyard.com

Fiskars®, Inc.
(800) 950-0203
www.fiskars.com

Flair® Designs
(888) 546-9990
www.flairdesignsinc.com

FloraCraft - no contact info

FontWerks
(604) 942-3105
www.fontwerks.com

FoofaLa
(402) 330-3208
www.foofala.com

Generations
(800) 905-1888
www.generationsnow.com

Hallmark Cards, Inc.
(800) 425-6275
www.hallmark.com

Heidi Swapp/Advantus
Corporation
(904) 482-0092
www.heidiswapp.com

Hero Arts® Rubber Stamps, Inc.
(800) 822-4376
www.heroarts.com

Hot Off The Press, Inc.
(800) 227-9595
www.paperpizazz.com

Hunt Corporation
(800) 879-4868
www.hunt-corp.com

Imagination Project, Inc.
(513) 860-2711
www.imaginationproject.com

Jest Charming
(702) 564-5101
www.jestcharming.com

JudiKins
(310) 515-1115
www.judikins.com

Junkitz™
(732) 792-1108
www.junkitz.com

K & Company
(888) 244-2083
www.kandcompany.com

Karen Foster Design
(801) 451-9779
www.karenfosterdesign.com

Keeping Memories Alive™
(800) 419-4949
www.scrapbooks.com

KI Memories
(972) 243-5595
www.kimemories.com

Kopp Design
(801) 489-6011
www.koppdesign.com

Krylon®
(216) 566-200
www.krylon.com

Lasting Impressions for Paper,
Inc.
(801) 298-1979
www.lastingimpressions.com

Li'l Davis Designs
(949) 838-0344
www.lildavisdesigns.com

Little Black Dress Designs
(360) 894-8844
www.littleblackdressdesigns.com

Magenta Rubber Stamps
(800) 565-5254
www.magentastyle.com

Magic Mesh
(651) 345-6374
www.magicmesh.com

Magic Scraps™
(972) 238-1838
www.magicscraps.com

Making Memories
(800) 286-5263
www.makingmemories.com

Marvy® Uchida/ Uchida of
America, Corp.
(800) 541-5877
www.uchida.com

Mary Engelbreit Studios, Inc.
(800) 443-MARY
www.maryengelbreit.com

May Arts
(800) 442-3950
www.mayarts.com

me & my BiG ideas®
(949) 883-2065
www.meandmybigideas.com

Memories Complete™, LLC
(866) 966-6365
www.memoriescomplete.com

Mustard Moon™
(408) 299-8542
www.mustardmoon.com

My Mind's Eye™, Inc.
(800) 665-5116
www.frame-ups.com

Office Depot
www.officedepot.com

Offray- see Berwick Offray, LLC

O'Scrap/Imaginations, Inc.
(801) 225-6015
www.imaginations-inc.com

Paper Adventures®
(800) 525-3196
www.paperadventures.com

Paper Company, The/ANW
Crestwood
(800) 525-3196
www.anwcrestwood.com

Paper Fever, Inc.
(800) 477-0902
www.paperfever.com

Paper Loft
(866) 254-1961
www.paperloft.com

Paper Palette LLC, The
(801) 849-8338
www.stickybackpaper.com

Paper Source
(888) paper-11
www.paper-source.com

Paper Studio- no contact info

Patchwork Paper Design, Inc.
(239) 433-4820
www.patchworkpaper.com

Pebbles Inc.
(801) 224-1857
www.pebblesinc.com

Plaid Enterprises, Inc.
(800) 842-4197
www.plaidonline.com

Prickley Pear Rubber Stamps
www.prickleypear.com

Prima Marketing, Inc.
(909) 627-5532
www.mulberrypaperflowers.com

Provo Craft®
(888) 577-3545
www.provocraft.com

PSX Design™
(800) 782-6748
www.psxdesign.com

QuicKutz, Inc.
(801) 765-1144
www.quickutz.com

QVC®
www.qvc.com

Ranger Industries, Inc.
(800) 244-2211
www.rangerink.com

Rusty Pickle
(801) 746-1045
www.rustypickle.com

Sandylion Sticker Designs
(800) 387-4215
www.sandylion.com

Scenic Route Paper Co.
(801) 785-0761
www.scenicroutepaper.com

ScrapArts
(503) 631-4893
www.scraparts.com

Scrapworks, LLC
(801) 363-1010
www.scrapworks.com

Scrapyard 329
(775) 829-1118
www.scrapyard329.com

SEI, Inc.
(800) 333-3279
www.shopsei.com

S.R.M. Press, Inc.
(800) 323-9589
www.srmpress.com

Stampendous!®
(800) 869-0474
www.stampendous.com

Sticker Studio™
(208) 322-2465
www.stickerstudio.com

Sweetwater
(800) 359-3094
www.sweetwaterscrapbook.com

Target
www.target.com

Ten Seconds Studio
(817) 428-0221
www.tensecondsstudio.com

Therm O Web, Inc.
(800) 323-0799
www.thermoweb.com

Tombow®
(800) 835-3232
www.tombowusa.com

Tsukineko®, Inc.
(800) 769-6633
www.tsukineko.com

Wal-Mart Stores, Inc.
(800) WALMART
www.walmart.com

Wendi Speciale Designs
www.wendispeciale.com

Westrim® Crafts
(800) 727-2727
www.westrimcrafts.com

Wrights® Ribbon Accents
(877) 597-4448
www.wrights.com

Index

Learn more with the authors of these fine titles from Memory Makers Books!

These books and other fine Memory Makers Books titles are available from your local art or craft retailer, bookstore or online supplier. Please see page 2 of this book for contact information for Canada, Australia, the U.K. and Europe.

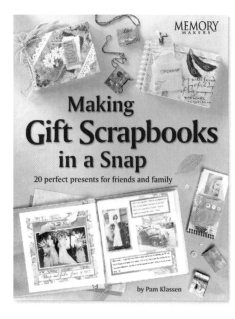

Making Gift Scrapbooks in a Snap
ISBN-13: 978-1892127-36-5,
ISBN-10: 1-89212-736-9,
paperback, 96 pgs., #32994

Memories in Miniature
ISBN-13: 978-1-892127-50-1,
ISBN-10: 1-89212-750-4,
paperback, 96 pgs., #33266

A Passion for Specialty Paper
ISBN-13: 978-1-892127-61-7,
ISBN-10: 1-892127-61-X,
paperback, 96 pgs., #33460

Creative Collage for Scrapbooks
ISBN-13: 978-1-892127-58-7,
ISBN-10: 1-892127-58-X,
paperback, 128 pgs., #33419